MW00917419

A Practical Guide To Digital Marketing

Elevate Your Brand and Drive Business Growth

Sebastian Pistritto

Copyright © **2024 Sebastian Pistritto**

All rights reserved. No part of this publication may be reproduced, distributed, or transmitted in any form or by any means without the prior written permission of the author.

Dedication

To my wife and our children. For always believing in me.

Cynthia Light Pistritto, Matthew Pistritto, Katie Pistritto and Daniel Pistritto

A PRACTICAL GUIDE TO DIGITAL MARKETING

Table of Contents

A PRACTICAL GUIDE TO DIGITAL MARKETING

Overview
Digital Marketing and Its Importance to a Business

Digital marketing has changed the way businesses connect with their audiences. As technology continues to advance, the scope and methods of digital marketing are expanding, offering businesses numerous opportunities to reach potential customers more effectively and efficiently. This comprehensive overview explores the key components of digital marketing and outlines the various benefits it offers to businesses of all sizes.

Digital marketing encompasses all marketing efforts that use an electronic device or the internet. It leverages online channels such as search engines, social media, email, and websites to connect with current and prospective customers. Unlike traditional marketing methods, digital marketing allows for more precise targeting, real-time analytics, and a higher level of engagement with audiences.

In this book, we will discuss the key components of digital marketing and how you can successfully implement them for your business.

We are going to explain the many benefits and some of the reasons why your business should be implementing digital marketing strategies. One of the most significant advantages of digital marketing is its cost-effectiveness. Compared to traditional marketing methods like print advertising or TV commercials, digital marketing channels are typically more affordable. Even small businesses with limited budgets can execute effective digital marketing campaigns.

A PRACTICAL GUIDE TO DIGITAL MARKETING

Digital marketing allows businesses to target specific demographics, interests, and behaviors. Tools such as social media advertising and PPC campaigns offer advanced targeting options that enable marketers to reach the right audience at the right time. Furthermore, personalized marketing messages can be crafted based on customer data, enhancing relevance and engagement.

Digital marketing provides measurable results through various analytics tools. Businesses can track key performance indicators (KPIs) such as website traffic, conversion rates, click-through rates, and engagement metrics. This data-driven approach allows for continuous improvement and optimization of marketing strategies.

Digital marketing facilitates two-way communication between businesses and their audiences. Social media platforms, in particular, allow for direct interactions through comments, likes, shares, and messages. This engagement helps build stronger relationships with customers and fosters brand loyalty.

The internet breaks down geographical barriers, allowing businesses to reach a global audience. Digital marketing campaigns can be tailored to target specific regions or languages, expanding a company's market reach and potential customer base.

With precise targeting and personalized messaging, digital marketing often results in higher conversion rates. Techniques such as A/B testing and retargeting campaigns further optimize conversion opportunities, ensuring that businesses maximize their return on investment (ROI).

Digital marketing campaigns can be easily adjusted based on performance data and changing market conditions. This flexibility allows businesses to adapt their strategies to meet evolving customer needs quickly. Additionally, digital marketing efforts can be scaled up or down as required, making it suitable for businesses of all sizes.

Digital marketing tools provide valuable insights into customer behavior and preferences. By analyzing data from various touchpoints, businesses can gain a deeper understanding of their audience, allowing for more informed decision-making and better marketing strategies.

Digital marketing levels the playing field, enabling small and medium-sized enterprises (SMEs) to compete with larger corporations. With the right strategies, smaller businesses can effectively reach and engage their target audience without requiring substantial financial resources.

A well-executed digital marketing strategy helps build brand awareness and credibility. Consistent online presence, valuable content, and positive customer reviews contribute to a trustworthy brand image. Social proof, such as testimonials and case studies, further enhances credibility.

Digital marketing offers a plethora of benefits for businesses, from cost-effectiveness and enhanced targeting to improved engagement and global reach. By leveraging digital marketing strategies, businesses can achieve significant growth, build strong relationships with customers, and stay competitive in the ever-changing market landscape. Embrace digital marketing to unlock your business's full potential and drive long-term success.

CHAPTER 1
Introduction to Digital Marketing

Digital marketing is the use of digital channels, platforms, and technologies to promote products, services, and brands to potential customers. Unlike traditional marketing methods that rely on physical mediums such as print, television, and radio, digital marketing leverages the internet and electronic devices to reach and engage a broader audience. It encompasses a wide range of strategies and practices designed to connect with consumers, build brand awareness, drive sales, and foster customer loyalty.

Digital marketing is a multifaceted discipline with several core components. Here are some of the primary elements:

Search Engine Optimization (SEO): SEO involves optimizing a website to rank higher in search engine results pages (SERPs). It focuses on improving the site's visibility to attract organic (non-paid) traffic. SEO practices include keyword research, on-page optimization, content creation, and link building.

Content Marketing: Content marketing is the creation and distribution of valuable, relevant content aimed at attracting and engaging a target audience. This includes blog posts, articles, videos, infographics, eBooks, and more. The goal is to provide useful information that addresses the needs and interests of potential customers.

Social Media Marketing (SMM): SMM involves using social media platforms like Facebook, Twitter, Instagram, LinkedIn, and others to promote products and services. It includes both organic efforts (such as regular posting and

1

community engagement) and paid advertising (such as sponsored posts and social ads).

Pay-Per-Click Advertising (PPC): PPC is a model of online advertising where advertisers pay a fee each time their ad is clicked. It is commonly used in search engine advertising (like Google Ads) and display advertising (banner ads on websites). PPC campaigns can be highly targeted and provide measurable results.

Email Marketing: Email marketing involves sending targeted emails to a list of subscribers. This can include newsletters, promotional offers, product announcements, and personalized messages. Email marketing is an effective way to nurture leads, build relationships, and drive conversions.

Affiliate Marketing: Affiliate marketing is a performance-based strategy where businesses reward affiliates (partners) for driving traffic or sales through their marketing efforts. Affiliates promote products using unique links, and they earn commissions for each sale or lead generated.

Influencer Marketing: Influencer marketing leverages individuals with a large and engaged following on social media or other digital platforms to promote products. Influencers create authentic content and endorse products, helping brands reach new audiences and build credibility.

Mobile Marketing: Mobile marketing targets users on smartphones and tablets through various channels, including mobile apps, SMS, MMS, and mobile websites. It also includes location-based marketing and mobile-optimized content.

Video Marketing: Video marketing involves creating and sharing videos to promote products, educate audiences, and entertain viewers. Platforms like YouTube, Vimeo, and social media are popular for video marketing. Videos enhance engagement and convey information effectively.

Analytics and Data Analysis: Digital marketing relies heavily on data and analytics to measure and analyze the performance of campaigns. Tools like Google Analytics provide insights into website traffic, user behavior, conversion rates, and other key metrics, allowing marketers to optimize their strategies.

Digital marketing has become an indispensable part of modern business strategies, offering a diverse range of tools and techniques to connect with audiences in meaningful ways. From the early days of basic websites and email marketing to the sophisticated, data-driven approaches of today, digital marketing continues to evolve rapidly. By understanding its key components, adopting effective strategies, leveraging essential tools, and staying abreast of future trends, businesses can navigate the dynamic digital landscape and achieve sustainable growth and success. As technology advances and consumer behaviors shift, the future of digital marketing promises to be even more exciting and transformative, providing endless opportunities for innovation and engagement.

Digital marketing is a dynamic and ever-evolving field that plays a crucial role in modern business strategies. It encompasses a wide range of techniques and tools designed to connect with audiences, build brand awareness, drive sales, and foster customer loyalty. By leveraging the power of digital channels and staying abreast of emerging trends, businesses can effectively navigate the digital landscape and achieve sustainable growth and success.

CHAPTER 2
Building Your Online Presence

Let's begin by talking about what you need to create your own online presence. Building a robust online presence for a business requires a strategic and comprehensive approach that integrates various digital marketing elements. Your business will need a website to promote your company and the products and services that you provide. The website is where most consumers look for and visit to not only find out about your business but also seek validation for your business. Your prospects will visit your business website to get contact information, detail information of your offerings, and customer reviews. So, having an online presence is critical to the success of your business. Here's a detailed guide on the essential steps and considerations for creating your online presence.

Build Your Brand Identity: Brand identity is a comprehensive set of characteristics and elements that a business uses to portray the right image to its consumers. It encompasses everything that makes a brand unique and recognizable, including its values, personality, voice, and visual elements. Brand identity is how a business wants to be perceived in the market and is distinct from brand image, which is how consumers perceive the brand and your business. When building your brand, consider the following:

- Mission and Values: Define what your business stands for.

- Visual Identity: Logo, color scheme, and design aesthetics.

4

- Voice and Tone: Consistent communication style across all channels.

Create a Professional Website for Business: A business website is a digital platform that represents a company or organization on the internet. It serves as a virtual storefront, providing information about the business, its products or services, and other essential details to both current and potential customers. A well-designed business website typically includes various sections, such as:

- Home Page: An overview of what the business offers and its core values.

- About Us: Information about the company's history, mission, vision, and team.

- Products/Services: Detailed descriptions of the products or services offered.

- Contact Us: Contact information, including address, phone number, email, and a contact form.

- Blog: Regularly updated articles and posts related to the business's industry.

- FAQ: Answers to common questions about the business and its offerings.

- Testimonials/Reviews: Customer feedback and success stories.

A website is often the first point of contact between a business and its potential customers. A professionally designed website establishes credibility and builds trust. It shows that the business is legitimate, well-established, and serious about its operations. In today's digital age, not having a website can make a business appear outdated or unreliable.

A PRACTICAL GUIDE TO DIGITAL MARKETING

A website makes a business accessible 24/7, allowing customers to find information about products or services at any time. It also enhances the business's visibility, as potential customers can discover the business through search engines, social media, and online advertising.

A website provides multiple ways for customers to interact with the business, including contact forms, live chat, and email subscriptions. It also allows the business to engage with customers through blogs, newsletters, and social media integration, fostering a stronger relationship and increasing customer loyalty.

A website is a central hub for all digital marketing and advertising efforts. It can host various marketing materials, such as landing pages, blogs, and case studies, and integrate with social media and email marketing campaigns. Additionally, a website is essential for search engine optimization (SEO), which helps improve the business's visibility on search engine results pages (SERPs).

For businesses that sell products or services online, a website is crucial for e-commerce. It allows customers to browse products, make purchases, and track orders conveniently. An e-commerce-enabled website can significantly expand a business's reach beyond its physical location, tapping into a global market.

A website allows businesses to collect and analyze data on customer behavior, preferences, and interactions. Tools like Google Analytics provide valuable insights into website traffic, user demographics, and engagement metrics. This data helps businesses make informed decisions, optimize their marketing strategies, and improve the overall customer experience.

A PRACTICAL GUIDE TO DIGITAL MARKETING

A website is an ideal platform to showcase a business's products or services in detail. High-quality images, videos, and detailed descriptions can highlight the features and benefits, helping potential customers make informed decisions. This detailed presentation is often more comprehensive than what can be achieved through other marketing channels.

A website can improve customer service by providing answers to common questions through FAQs, tutorials, and support pages. Features like live chat and contact forms allow customers to reach out for assistance easily, ensuring that their needs are addressed promptly.

A website is a powerful tool for building and reinforcing brand awareness. Consistent branding elements, such as logos, color schemes, and messaging, create a cohesive brand identity that customers recognize and remember. Regularly updated content and a strong online presence keep the brand top-of-mind for customers.

In most industries, having a website is essential to remain competitive. Many of your customers will research online before making purchasing decisions, and a lack of an online presence can result in lost opportunities to competitors who have well-established websites. A website allows businesses to compete on a level playing field, regardless of their size or location.

A business website is an essential tool in the digital age, providing numerous benefits, from establishing credibility to enhancing customer engagement and supporting marketing efforts. By integrating various features and focusing on user experience, a business can create a powerful online presence that drives growth and success. Investing in a well-designed website is not just an option but a necessity for any business aiming to thrive in today's competitive market.

Best Practice: Create a User-Friendly and Intuitive Navigation Structure

- **User Personas:** Develop detailed user personas to understand the needs, preferences, and behaviors of your target audience.

- **User Flow Mapping:** Map out the typical user journey from entry to conversion. Identify the key pages users are likely to visit and the actions they will take.

- **Primary Navigation:** Limit the primary navigation menu to the most important sections of your site (e.g., Home, About, Services, Products, Contact).

- **Dropdown Menus:** Use dropdown menus for secondary options but avoid overloading them with too many choices. Keep it simple and organized.

- **Clear Labels:** Use clear and descriptive labels for menu items that convey the content and purpose of each section. Avoid jargon and ambiguous terms.

- **SEO Optimization:** Incorporate relevant keywords into your navigation labels to enhance SEO while maintaining clarity.

- **Uniform Design:** Maintain a consistent design and layout for navigation across all pages to avoid confusing users.

- **Predictable Locations:** Place the navigation menu in a predictable location (typically at the top or on the left side of the page) where users expect to find it.

- **Search Bar:** Include a prominently placed search bar to help users quickly find specific information.

- **Autocomplete Feature:** Use autocomplete to provide suggestions as users type, enhancing the search experience.

- **Responsive Design:** Ensure the navigation menu is mobile-friendly, with a design that adapts to different screen sizes.

- **Hamburger Menu:** Use a hamburger menu (three horizontal lines) for mobile devices to keep the interface clean and accessible.

- **Call-to-Action (CTA):** Use CTAs to guide users to important pages such as services, products, or contact forms.

- **Visual Cues:** Use visual cues like buttons, icons, or highlighted text to draw attention to key navigation elements.

- **User Testing:** Conduct usability testing to gather feedback on the navigation structure from real users.

- **Heatmaps and Analytics:** Use heatmaps and website analytics to understand user behavior and identify areas for improvement.

- **A/B Testing:** Perform A/B testing on different navigation layouts and structures to determine the most effective setup.

By focusing on creating a user-friendly and intuitive navigation structure, you make it easier for visitors to navigate your site, find what they are looking for, and engage with your content. This leads to a more satisfying user experience and increases the likelihood of achieving your business goals.

Your Business Needs to Have a Social Media Presence.

A social media presence refers to a business's active participation and visibility on social media platforms such as Facebook, Twitter, Instagram, LinkedIn, TikTok, and others. It involves creating and managing accounts on these platforms, posting regular content, engaging with the audience, and using social media tools to promote the brand. A strong social media presence enables businesses to connect with their customers, build brand awareness, and drive engagement and sales. A business with a Social Media Presence can benefit in the following ways:

Enhanced Brand Awareness and Reach: Social media platforms have billions of users worldwide, offering businesses an unparalleled opportunity to reach a vast audience. By maintaining an active presence, businesses can increase their visibility, making it easier for potential customers to discover and recognize their brand.

- **Example:** A local bakery uses Instagram to post photos of their freshly baked goods, reaching food enthusiasts and potential customers beyond their immediate geographic area.

Improved Customer Engagement and Interaction: Social media provides a direct line of communication between businesses and their customers. Through comments, messages, and live interactions, businesses can engage with their audience, answer questions, address concerns, and gather valuable feedback.

- **Example**: A tech company uses Twitter to provide customer support, respond to queries and resolve issues quickly, thereby improving customer satisfaction and loyalty.

Cost-Effective Marketing and Advertising: Social media marketing is generally more affordable than traditional advertising methods. Platforms like Facebook, Instagram, and LinkedIn offer targeted advertising options that allow businesses to reach specific demographics, interests, and behaviors, maximizing their marketing budget.

- **Example**: A new e-commerce store runs targeted Facebook ads to reach users interested in online shopping and specific product categories, driving traffic to their website at a lower cost than traditional ads.

Content Distribution and Promotion: Social media is an effective channel for distributing and promoting content. Whether it's blog posts, videos, infographics, or updates, social media helps businesses share their content with a broader audience, driving traffic to their website and increasing engagement.

- **Example**: A fashion brand uses Instagram Stories to showcase new collections, behind-the-scenes content, and styling tips, driving interest and engagement with their products.

Building a Community and Brand Loyalty: Social media allows businesses to build a community around their brand. By consistently posting valuable content and engaging with followers, businesses can foster a sense of loyalty and connection, turning customers into brand advocates.

- **Example**: A fitness company creates a Facebook group where members can share their progress, ask questions, and support each other, building a loyal community around their brand.

Market Insights and Customer Feedback: Social media platforms offer tools and analytics that provide valuable insights into customer behavior, preferences, and trends. Businesses can use this data to refine their strategies, improve products or services, and better understand their audience.

- **Example**: A restaurant monitors Instagram engagement to see which menu items are most popular among their followers, allowing them to make data-driven decisions about their offerings.

Enhanced SEO and Online Presence: An active social media presence can improve a business's search engine ranking. Social media profiles often appear in search engine results, and links shared on social platforms can drive traffic to the business's website, boosting its SEO performance.

- **Example**: A travel agency shares blog posts about travel tips and destinations on social media, driving traffic to their website and improving their search engine rankings.

Competitive Advantage: In today's digital age, having a social media presence is essential for staying competitive. Businesses that effectively leverage social media can differentiate themselves from competitors, attract more customers, and retain existing ones.

- **Example**: A startup uses LinkedIn to share industry insights and thought leadership content, positioning itself as an expert and gaining a competitive edge over fewer active competitors.

Crisis Management and Reputation Control: Social media allows businesses to manage their reputation and respond quickly to any crises or negative feedback. Timely and transparent communication can mitigate damage and maintain customer trust.

- **Example**: An airline uses Twitter to provide real-time updates and responses during a flight disruption, addressing customer concerns and maintaining its reputation.

Best Practice: Develop a Consistent and Authentic Brand Voice

Creating a strong social media presence for your business involves several elements, but one of the most crucial is developing a consistent and authentic brand voice. This ensures that your business is recognizable and relatable across all social media platforms, helping to build trust and engagement with your audience.

Steps to Develop a Consistent and Authentic Brand Voice

1. **Define Your Brand Voice:**

   o **Brand Personality:** Determine the personality traits of your brand. Is it professional, casual, playful, authoritative, compassionate, etc.?

   o **Values and Mission:** Reflect your company's core values and mission in your tone of voice. This should align with your business's overall messaging and marketing strategy.

o **Audience Expectations:** Understand how your audience expects to be communicated with. This can vary significantly depending on your industry and target demographic.

2. **Create a Style Guide:**

o **Tone and Style:** Document guidelines for tone and style, including word choices, sentence structures, and preferred topics. For example, a financial consulting firm may use a formal tone, while a lifestyle brand might adopt a more casual and friendly tone.

o **Visual Elements:** Include visual guidelines such as color schemes, fonts, and imagery styles that should be used consistently across posts.

o **Do's and Don'ts:** List out examples of appropriate and inappropriate content, including how to handle sensitive topics or customer complaints.

3. **Train Your Team:**

o **Unified Understanding:** Ensure that everyone involved in creating content understands and adheres to the brand voice guidelines.

o **Workshops and Resources:** Conduct workshops and provide resources to help your team internalize the brand voice. Use real-life examples and practice scenarios.

4. **Consistent Messaging Across Platforms:**

o **Platform Adaptation:** Adapt your messaging style to fit the specific social media platform while maintaining your core brand voice. For instance,

LinkedIn might require a more professional tone compared to Instagram.

o **Cross-Posting Strategy:** If you are cross-posting content across multiple platforms, adjust the messaging slightly to fit the nuances of each platform while keeping the core message consistent.

5. **Engage Authentically:**

o **Genuine Interaction:** Engage with your audience authentically. Respond to comments, messages, and reviews in a manner that reflects your brand voice.

o **Human Touch:** Show the human side of your brand by sharing behind-the-scenes content, employee stories, or user-generated content. This builds a more personal connection with your audience.

6. **Monitor and Adjust:**

o **Social Listening:** Use social listening tools to monitor how your audience responds to your content and voice. This helps in understanding the sentiment and adjusting the strategy if needed.

o **Feedback Loops:** Encourage and listen to feedback from your audience and team to continuously refine and improve your brand voice.

7. **Content Calendar and Consistency:**

o **Regular Posting:** Maintain a consistent posting schedule using a content calendar. This ensures that your audience knows when to expect new content from you.

- o **Diverse Content Mix:** Plan a mix of content types that align with your brand voice, such as educational posts, product updates, behind-the-scenes content, and customer stories.

- o **Genuine Interaction:** Respond to comments with a friendly and helpful tone, addressing customer queries and thanking them for positive feedback.

- o **Human Touch:** Share photos and stories of the team, behind-the-scenes looks at product sourcing, and user-generated content.

By following these steps and focusing on a consistent and authentic brand voice, you can create a strong and engaging social media presence that resonates with your audience and supports your business goals.

A robust social media presence is vital for modern businesses. It enhances brand awareness, improves customer engagement, supports cost-effective marketing, and provides valuable insights. By leveraging social media effectively, businesses can build a strong online presence, foster community and loyalty, and gain a competitive edge in their industry. Whether through targeted ads, engaging content, or responsive customer service, social media is an essential tool for achieving business growth and success in today's digital landscape.

CHAPTER 3
Understanding Search Engine Optimization

Now that you have created an online presence for your business with a professional website, you need to promote it and attract customers and prospects so that they can visit the website and learn about you, your business and your products and services.

Search Engine Optimization (SEO) is the process of optimizing a website to improve its visibility and ranking on search engine results pages (SERPs). The goal of SEO is to attract more organic (non-paid) traffic to a website by making it more attractive to search engines like Google, Bing, and Yahoo. Here are a few reasons why you need SEO for your business.

Increased Visibility and Traffic: SEO helps your website appear higher in search engine results, making it more likely that users will visit your site. Higher visibility in search results translates to increased organic traffic, which is crucial for attracting potential customers.

- **Example**: A local bakery optimizing for keywords like "best bakery in [city]" can appear in the top results when someone searches for bakeries in their area, driving more foot traffic to their shop.

Cost-Effective Marketing Tool: Compared to paid advertising, SEO is a cost-effective marketing strategy. While it requires time and effort, the organic traffic generated through SEO does not incur a direct cost per click, making it a sustainable long-term investment.

- **Example**: An online retailer can reduce its reliance on paid ads by consistently appearing in organic search results for product-related queries, saving on advertising costs.

Enhanced User Experience when Visiting Your Website: SEO involves optimizing your website's content, structure, and performance, which collectively enhances the user experience. A well-optimized site is faster, easier to navigate, and more informative, leading to higher user satisfaction.

- **Example**: A news website optimizing its loading speed and mobile experience will retain more visitors, reducing bounce rates and increasing page views.

Building Credibility and Trust for the Business: Websites that rank higher in search results are often perceived as more credible and trustworthy. Users trust search engines to provide relevant and reliable results, so appearing at the top can enhance your brand's reputation.

- **Example**: A healthcare provider ranking high for "best pediatrician in [city]" is likely to be trusted more by potential patients compared to lower-ranked competitors.

Competitive Advantage: In competitive industries, businesses with strong SEO strategies can outperform their rivals in search results. By investing in SEO, you can gain an edge over competitors who may not be as focused on their search engine visibility.

- **Example**: A small law firm using SEO to rank highly for local legal services can attract clients who would otherwise go to larger, less optimized firms.

Local SEO for Local Businesses: For businesses that operate locally, local SEO is crucial. Optimizing for local search queries ensures that your business appears in local search results, Google Maps, and local business directories.

- **Example**: A restaurant optimizing for "Italian restaurant near me" will attract local diners looking for nearby dining options.

Informed Decision Making: SEO provides valuable data and insights into user behavior, search trends, and website performance. This information can guide your marketing strategies, content creation, and business decisions.

- **Example**: An e-commerce site analyzing SEO data to understand which products are most searched for can adjust its inventory and marketing efforts accordingly.

SEO is a vital component of a successful digital marketing strategy. It increases visibility, drives organic traffic, and enhances user experience, all of which contributes to higher conversions and business growth. By investing in SEO, businesses can build credibility, gain a competitive advantage, and make informed decisions based on valuable insights. In an increasingly digital world, a strong SEO strategy is essential for any business looking to succeed online.

SEO involves a variety of techniques and strategies that can be broadly categorized into on-page SEO, off-page SEO, and technical SEO. If you are technical or would like to explore how to implement SEO tactics on your website, below are some basic things to consider. This involves optimizing individual web pages to rank higher and earn more relevant traffic from search engines. This includes optimizing both the content and the HTML source code of a page. The primary components of on-page SEO are:

Content Quality and Relevance: High-quality content is the cornerstone of on-page SEO. Search engines prioritize content that provides value to users, is well-written, and is relevant to the search query.

- **Informative and Engaging:** Content should be informative, engaging, and useful to the target audience. It should answer users' questions and fulfill their search intent.

- **Original and Unique:** Avoid duplicate content. Ensure that your content is original and offers a unique perspective.

- **Comprehensive:** Cover the topic in-depth. Comprehensive content tends to perform better as it provides more value to the user.

Keyword Optimization: Keywords are the terms and phrases that users enter into search engines. Optimizing your content with relevant keywords helps search engines understand what your page is about.

- **Keyword Research:** Use tools like Google Keyword Planner, Ahrefs, or SEMrush to find relevant keywords with a good balance of search volume and competition.

- **Keyword Placement:** Integrate keywords naturally within the content, including the following:
  - Title tag
  - Headings and subheadings
  - Body content
  - Meta descriptions

    o   URL

    o   Image alt text

Title Tags: The title tag is an HTML element that specifies the title of a web page. It is one of the most important on-page SEO factors.

- **Include Keywords**: Incorporate primary keywords towards the beginning of the title.

- **Length**: Keep the title tag under 60 characters to ensure it displays correctly in search results.

- **Descriptive and Compelling**: Make the title descriptive and compelling to encourage clicks.

Meta Descriptions: The meta description is a summary of a web page's content that appears under the title in search results.

- **Include Keywords**: Include relevant keywords but avoid keyword stuffing.

- **Length**: Keep it between 150-160 characters to ensure its fully displayed in search results.

- **Engaging**: Write an engaging meta description that encourages users to click on the link.

Headings (H1, H2, H3, etc.): Headings help organize content and make it easier for users and search engines to understand the structure of the content.

- **H1 Tag**: Use one H1 tag per page as the main title. It should include the primary keyword.

- **Subheadings (H2, H3, etc.)**: Use H2 tags for main sections and H3 tags for subsections. Include relevant keywords in these headings to improve SEO and readability.

URL Structure: A clean and descriptive URL structure helps search engines and users understand what the page is about.

- **Include Keywords**: Use keywords in the URL but keep it concise.

- **Readability**: Ensure the URL is readable and avoid using unnecessary numbers or characters.

- **Hyphens for Separation**: Use hyphens (-) to separate words in the URL.

Internal Linking: Internal links are links from one page on your website to another page on the same site. They help establish a hierarchy and spread link equity (ranking power) around websites.

- **Relevant Anchor Text**: Use descriptive and relevant anchor text for internal links.

- **Link to Related Content**: Link to related content to provide additional value to users and improve site navigation.

- **Balance**: Ensure a balance of internal links to avoid over-optimization.

Image Optimization: Images should be optimized to enhance page load speed and improve SEO.

- **Alt Text**: Use descriptive, keyword-rich alt text to help search engines understand the image content.

- **File Names**: Use descriptive file names with keywords separated by hyphens.

- **File Size**: Compress images to reduce file size without sacrificing quality, improving page load speed.

Mobile-Friendliness: With the increasing use of mobile devices, ensuring your website is mobile-friendly is crucial for SEO.

- **Responsive Design**: Use responsive design to ensure your site adapts to different screen sizes.

- **Mobile Usability**: Ensure buttons and links are easily clickable and text is readable without zooming.

Page Load Speed: Page load speed is a critical factor for user experience and SEO. Faster pages provide a better user experience and can improve search rankings.

- **Optimize Images**: Compress images and use appropriate file formats.

- **Minimize HTTP Requests**: Reduce the number of elements on your page to minimize HTTP requests.

- **Use Browser Caching**: Enable browser caching to speed up page load times for repeat visitors.

- **Minify CSS and JavaScript**: Reduce the size of your CSS and JavaScript files by removing unnecessary spaces and comments.

Content Freshness: Regularly updating your content can improve its relevance and ranking potential.

- **Update Old Content**: Revise and update old content to keep it relevant and accurate.

- **Add New Information**: Include new information, data, or insights to enhance the value of the content.

User Experience (UX): A positive user experience encourages longer visits and higher engagement, which can positively impact SEO.

- **Ease of Navigation:** Ensure your site is easy to navigate with a clear structure and menu.

- **Readable Content:** Use a clean design with easy-to-read fonts, short paragraphs, and plenty of white space.

- **Engagement Features:** Include features like comments, social sharing buttons, and related content to encourage user interaction.

Best Practice: Conduct Comprehensive Keyword Research and Optimization

Conducting comprehensive keyword research and optimizing your website's content accordingly is a fundamental best practice for optimizing SEO for your business. This process involves identifying the most relevant and valuable keywords your target audience is searching for and strategically incorporating these keywords into your website to improve search engine rankings.

Steps to Conduct Comprehensive Keyword Research and Optimization

1. Understand Your Audience and Market

- **Audience Analysis:** Identify your target audience's demographics, interests, pain points, and search behavior.

- **Competitor Analysis:** Analyze your competitors' websites to understand which keywords they are targeting and performing well for.

2. Use Keyword Research Tools

- **Google Keyword Planner:** Utilize this tool to discover keyword ideas and get search volume data.

- **Ahrefs:** Analyze keyword difficulty, search volume, and related keywords to prioritize your efforts.

- **SEMrush:** Conduct comprehensive keyword research, competitive analysis, and find keyword gaps.

- **Moz Keyword Explorer:** Get keyword suggestions, analyze search volume, and find opportunities for long-tail keywords.

3. Identify and Prioritize Keywords

- **Relevant Keywords:** Focus on keywords that are highly relevant to your business, products, or services.

- **Search Volume:** Target keywords with a significant search volume to ensure you are optimizing for terms that users are actively searching for.

- **Keyword Difficulty:** Consider the competition level for each keyword and prioritize those with a balance of search volume and lower competition.

- **Long-Tail Keywords:** Incorporate long-tail keywords (specific phrases) as they often have lower competition and higher conversion rates.

4. Create High-Quality, Optimized Content

- **Content Strategy:** Develop a content strategy that addresses your audience's needs and incorporates your targeted keywords.

- **On-Page Optimization:**

o **Title Tags:** Include primary keywords naturally in your title tags.

o **Headings:** Use H1, H2, and H3 tags to structure content and include keywords where appropriate.

o **Meta Descriptions:** Write compelling meta descriptions that include target keywords to improve click-through rates.

o **URL Structure:** Use clean and keyword-rich URLs.

o **Keyword Density:** Naturally incorporate keywords throughout the content without keyword stuffing.

- **Content Quality:** Ensure your content is informative, engaging, and valuable to your audience.

5. Optimize Technical SEO

- **Site Speed:** Improve page load times by optimizing images, leveraging browser caching, and minimizing HTTP requests.

- **Mobile Optimization:** Ensure your website is fully responsive and offers a seamless experience on mobile devices.

- **Secure Website:** Use HTTPS to secure your site and improve trustworthiness.

- **XML Sitemap:** Create and submit an XML sitemap to help search engines crawl your site more efficiently.

- **Robots.txt:** Use the robots.txt file to guide search engine crawlers on which pages to index.

6. Build Quality Backlinks

- **Guest Blogging:** Write guest posts on reputable sites within your industry to earn backlinks.

- **Content Marketing:** Create shareable and link-worthy content such as infographics, guides, and research reports.

- **Outreach:** Reach out to influencers, bloggers, and websites to promote your content and gain backlinks.

7. Monitor and Analyze Performance

- **Google Analytics:** Track organic traffic, user behavior, and conversions.

- **Google Search Console:** Monitor search performance index coverage and fix crawl errors.

- **SEO Tools:** Use tools like Ahrefs, SEMrush, and Moz to track keyword rankings, backlinks, and site performance.

Search Engine Optimization is essential for improving your website's visibility and ranking in search engine results. By focusing on content quality, keyword optimization, meta tags, headings, URL structure, internal linking, image optimization, mobile-friendliness, page load speed, content freshness, and user experience, you can create a well-optimized website that attracts and retains visitors. Implementing these on-page SEO components effectively will help your business achieve higher search engine rankings, drive more organic traffic, and ultimately increase conversions and revenue.

CHAPTER 4
Understand and Leverage Content Marketing

What is Content Marketing

Content marketing is a strategic marketing approach focused on creating, publishing, and distributing valuable, relevant, and consistent content to attract and engage a clearly defined audience—and, ultimately, to drive profitable customer action. Unlike traditional marketing, which often interrupts potential customers with advertisements, content marketing aims to provide valuable information that helps solve problems or meets the needs of the audience.

Examples of Content Marketing Include:

o **Blogs**: Articles that provide insights, information, and answers to questions that the target audience is searching for.

o **Videos**: Visual content that can range from tutorials and product demonstrations to behind-the-scenes looks and interviews.

o **Infographics**: Visual representations of data and information that make complex topics easy to understand.

o **ebooks and Whitepapers**: In-depth resources that provide comprehensive information on specific topics.

o **Podcasts**: Audio content that offers convenience for audiences to listen to expert discussions and interviews on-the-go.

o **Social Media Posts**: Short, engaging content that drives interaction on platforms like Facebook, Twitter, Instagram, and LinkedIn.

Benefits of Content Marketing

Content marketing is crucial for businesses today due to its multifaceted benefits that extend beyond traditional marketing approaches. Here are several key reasons why content marketing is important for business:

Increased Brand Awareness: Content marketing helps businesses increase their visibility and reach a broader audience. By consistently creating and sharing valuable content, businesses can make their brand more recognizable and memorable.

- **Example**: A fashion retailer regularly publishes blog posts on the latest trends, which not only showcases their expertise but also attracts potential customers looking for style advice.

Improved Search Engine Rankings: Search engines favor high-quality, relevant content. By optimizing your content for SEO, you can improve your website's search engine rankings, making it easier for potential customers to find you.

- **Example**: A tech company creates in-depth guides on using their software, which ranks well on Google and drives organic traffic to their site.

Enhanced Audience Engagement: Engaging content keeps your audience interested and encourages them to interact with your brand. This can lead to increased loyalty and stronger relationships with customers.

- **Example**: A food brand shares recipes and cooking tips on social media, prompting followers to comment with their own tips and questions, fostering a community around the brand.

Lead Generation and Conversion: Content marketing is effective for attracting and converting leads. By providing valuable information that addresses the needs and pain points of your audience, you can guide them through the buyer's journey.

- **Example**: A financial services company offers free ebooks on investment strategies in exchange for email sign-ups, generating leads that can be nurtured into clients.

Cost-Effective Marketing: Compared to traditional advertising methods, content marketing can be more cost-effective. Once created, high-quality content continues to attract and convert leads over time, providing ongoing value.

- **Example**: A small business publishes evergreen blog posts that continue to drive traffic and generate leads years after their initial publication.

Building Trust and Authority: Consistently producing valuable content helps establish your business as an authority in your industry. This builds trust with your audience, making them more likely to choose your products or services.

- **Example**: A healthcare provider regularly posts articles on health tips and wellness advice, positioning themselves as a trusted source of information.

Support for Other Marketing Strategies: Content marketing complements and enhances other marketing strategies, including social media marketing, email marketing, and paid advertising. High-quality content can be repurposed across various channels to maximize its impact.

- **Example**: A B2B company creates a comprehensive whitepaper and then uses snippets from it for social media posts, email campaigns, and even paid ads.

Improved Customer Retention: By continuously providing valuable content, businesses can keep their audience engaged and coming back for more. This helps in maintaining customer relationships and increasing lifetime value.

- **Example**: A subscription service sends regular newsletters with tips on how to get the most out of their product, keeping subscribers engaged and reducing churn.

Informed Decision Making: Content marketing provides insights into what resonates with your audience. By analyzing engagement metrics, you can better understand customer preferences and refine your marketing strategies accordingly.

- **Example**: An e-commerce site tracks which blog posts generate the most interest and adjusts its content strategy to focus on similar topics.

Competitive Advantage: In today's digital landscape, having a strong content marketing strategy can set you apart from competitors who may not be as focused on content. This can lead to increased market share and a stronger brand presence.

- **Example**: A real estate agency that publishes detailed market analysis reports and neighborhood guides can attract more clients than a competitor that doesn't provide such resources.

Best Practice: Develop a Comprehensive Content Marketing Strategy

Creating and using content marketing effectively involves a strategic approach that aligns your content efforts with your business goals, target audience needs, and available resources. Here's a detailed best practice guide on how to develop and implement a comprehensive content marketing strategy for your business:

Steps to Develop a Comprehensive Content Marketing Strategy

1. Define Your Goals and Objectives

- **Business Goals:** Align your content marketing efforts with your overall business goals (e.g., brand awareness, lead generation, customer retention).

- **SMART Objectives:** Set Specific, Measurable, Achievable, Relevant, and Time-bound objectives to track your progress and success.

2. Understand Your Target Audience

- **Buyer Personas:** Create detailed buyer personas that represent your ideal customers, including their demographics, interests, pain points, and behavior.

- **Audience Segmentation:** Segment your audience based on their needs and preferences to tailor your content more effectively.

3. Conduct a Content Audit

- **Existing Content:** Review your existing content to identify what's working, what's not, and where there are gaps.

- **Content Performance:** Use analytics to assess the performance of your current content in terms of engagement, conversions, and SEO.

4. Develop a Content Plan

- **Content Themes:** Identify key themes and topics that resonate with your audience and align with your business objectives.

- **Content Types:** Plan a mix of content types (e.g., blog posts, videos, infographics, eBooks, webinars) to keep your audience engaged.

- **Content Calendar:** Create a content calendar to schedule and organize your content production and publishing efforts.

5. Create High-Quality Content

- **Value-Driven Content:** Focus on creating content that provides real value to your audience, such as educational, entertaining, or inspiring material.

- **SEO Optimization:** Optimize your content for search engines by incorporating relevant keywords, meta descriptions, and internal links.

- **Visuals and Media:** Use high-quality visuals, videos, and infographics to enhance your content and make it more engaging.

6. Distribute and Promote Your Content

- **Owned Channels:** Use your website, blog, email newsletters, and social media profiles to distribute your content.

- **Earned Media:** Leverage PR, guest blogging, and influencer partnerships to reach a broader audience.

- **Paid Promotion:** Use paid channels like social media ads, Google Ads, and sponsored content to amplify your reach.

7. Engage with Your Audience

- **Social Media Interaction:** Actively engage with your audience on social media by responding to comments, messages, and mentions.

- **Community Building:** Foster a community around your brand by encouraging user-generated content, hosting webinars, and creating discussion forums.

8. Measure and Analyze Results

- **Analytics Tools:** Use tools like Google Analytics, HubSpot, and social media analytics to track the performance of your content.

- **KPIs:** Monitor key performance indicators (KPIs) such as traffic, engagement, conversion rates, and ROI.

- **Feedback Loop:** Gather feedback from your audience and stakeholders to continuously improve your content strategy.

9. Iterate and Improve

- **Regular Reviews:** Regularly review and update your content strategy based on performance data and feedback.

- **A/B Testing:** Conduct A/B testing on different content formats, headlines, and distribution channels to optimize your efforts.

- **Stay Updated:** Keep up with industry trends and evolving audience preferences to ensure your content remains relevant and effective.

Content marketing is an essential strategy in today's digital landscape. By focusing on creating and distributing valuable, relevant, and consistent content, businesses can attract and retain a clearly defined audience, drive profitable customer action, and achieve long-term success. Whether through blogs, videos, infographics, or social media posts, content marketing provides numerous benefits, including increased brand awareness, improved search engine rankings, enhanced audience engagement, and more. Implementing a robust content marketing strategy is crucial for any business looking to thrive in a competitive market.

CHAPTER 5
Digital Advertising

Digital advertising, also known as online advertising, refers to the practice of promoting products, services, or brands through digital channels such as websites, social media platforms, search engines, mobile apps, and email. Unlike traditional advertising, which includes mediums like print, radio, and television, digital advertising leverages the internet and digital technologies to deliver targeted and measurable promotional content to a specific audience.

Digital advertising has become a vital component of modern marketing strategies due to its ability to reach a vast and targeted audience, offer measurable results, and provide cost-effective solutions. Here's a detailed explanation of why digital advertising is essential for promoting your business:

Targeted Reach: Digital advertising allows businesses to precisely target their ideal audience based on various factors such as demographics, interests, behaviors, and geographic locations. This ensures that the most relevant people see your promotional messages.

- Example: A local restaurant can target ads to users within a specific radius who have shown interest in dining out, increasing the likelihood of attracting nearby customers.

Measurable Results: One of the significant advantages of digital advertising is the ability to track and measure the performance of your campaigns in real-time. Metrics such as impressions, clicks, conversions, and ROI provide valuable insights into the effectiveness of your ads.

- Example: An e-commerce business can track the number of clicks and conversions from a Facebook ad campaign, allowing them to calculate the exact cost per acquisition and adjust their budget accordingly.

Cost-Effectiveness: Digital advertising offers various budgeting options, from pay-per-click (PPC) models to fixed budgets for social media ads, making it accessible for businesses of all sizes. You can start with a small budget and scale up as you see the results.

- Example: A startup can launch a Google Ads campaign with a limited daily budget and increase spending gradually as they see a positive return on investment.

Enhanced Engagement: Interactive and multimedia ad formats such as video ads, carousel ads, and rich media ads can significantly increase user engagement and interaction with your brand. Engaging content encourages users to spend more time with your brand and take action.

- Example: A fitness brand uses Instagram Stories ads to showcase workout routines and engage users with polls and swipe-up links to sign up for classes.

Global Reach: Digital advertising breaks down geographic barriers, allowing businesses to reach a global audience. This is particularly beneficial for businesses looking to expand their market presence internationally.

- Example: An online software company can target potential customers worldwide through Google Ads and LinkedIn campaigns, extending its reach beyond local markets.

Real-Time Optimization: Digital advertising platforms offer the flexibility to make real-time adjustments to your campaigns. You can tweak ad creatives, targeting options, and budgets based on performance data to maximize effectiveness.

- Example: A fashion retailer notices that certain ads perform better in the evening and adjusts their campaign schedule to allocate more budget during peak engagement times.

Building Brand Awareness: Consistent and strategic digital advertising helps build brand awareness by keeping your business top-of-mind for potential customers. Over time, repeated exposure to your brand through various digital channels strengthens brand recognition and trust.

- Example: A tech startup uses display ads across popular tech blogs and YouTube channels to build brand awareness among tech enthusiasts and early adopters.

Supporting Other Marketing Strategies: Digital advertising complements and enhances other marketing efforts, such as content marketing, social media marketing, and email marketing. By promoting your content, offers, and events through digital ads, you can drive more traffic and engagement across all channels.

- Example: A beauty brand runs Facebook ads to promote a new blog post about skincare tips, driving traffic to their website and encouraging readers to subscribe to their newsletter for more tips.

Competitor Analysis and Advantage: Digital advertising platforms provide insights into competitor activities and allow you to stay competitive by analyzing their strategies. You can identify gaps and opportunities to differentiate your business and gain a competitive edge.

- Example: A travel agency uses SEMrush to monitor competitors' keyword strategies and bid on similar keywords to capture potential customers searching for vacation packages.

10. Scalability and Flexibility: Digital advertising campaigns are highly scalable, allowing you to start small and expand as your business grows. The flexibility to adjust campaigns based on performance and changing business goals makes digital advertising a dynamic tool.

- Example: An online course provider starts with a small budget targeting a niche audience and gradually scales up their ad spend as they acquire more students and expand their course offerings.

Now let's look at several different types of Digital Advertising for you to consider helping to promote your business.

- **Search Engine Pay-Per-Click (PPC)**: Advertisers pay each time a user clicks on their ad. This is commonly seen in search engine results pages (SERPs) like Google AdWords.

- **Search Engine Marketing (SEM)**: A broader strategy that includes PPC and other search engine advertising tactics to increase visibility on SERPs.

- **Display Advertising: Banner Ads**: Visual advertisements are displayed on websites, usually in the form of images, videos, or interactive media.

- **Rich Media Ads**: Interactive ads that engage users with elements like video, audio, or other multimedia.

- **Social Media Advertising: Sponsored Posts**: Paid content promoted on social media platforms to reach a broader audience.

- **Social Media Ads**: Various ad formats are available on platforms like Facebook, Instagram, Twitter, LinkedIn, and TikTok, including carousel ads, video ads, and story ads.

- **Video Advertising:** Ads that play before, during, or after video content on platforms like YouTube.

- **Native Advertising**
  - **Sponsored Content**: Ads that match the form and function of the platform on which they appear, making them look like regular content.
  - **Advertorials**: Articles or posts written in the style of editorial content but sponsored by an advertiser.

- **Affiliate Marketing**
  - **Performance-Based Ads**: Advertisers pay affiliates (partners) a commission for driving traffic or sales through their referral links.

- **Email Marketing**
  - Promotional Emails: Direct marketing messages sent to a list of subscribers or potential customers.
  - Retargeting Emails: Emails sent to users who have interacted with the brand but have not completed a desired action, like making a purchase.

- **Mobile Advertising**

- o In-App Ads: Advertisements displayed within mobile apps.

- o SMS Marketing: Promotional messages sent via text message.

- **Programmatic Advertising**

- o Automated Ad Buying: Using software to purchase digital advertising, often in real-time, to target specific audiences more efficiently.

Managing digital advertising comes with several challenges that marketers and business owners need to navigate to ensure the effectiveness and efficiency of their campaigns.

Ad Fatigue Challenges: Ad fatigue occurs when users see the same ad too frequently, leading to decreased engagement and annoyance. Overexposure to the same message can result in lower click-through rates (CTR) and conversion rates.

Solution: To combat ad fatigue, marketers should:

- Rotate ad creatives regularly to keep the content fresh and engaging.

- Use frequency capping to limit the number of times an individual sees the same ad.

- Segment audiences and tailor different messages to different segments.

Ad Blockers from Different Web Browsers: The use of ad blockers is increasing, which prevents ads from being displayed to users who have them installed. This reduces the reach and potential impact of digital advertising campaigns.

Solution: To address ad blockers, marketers can:

- Create non-intrusive, high-quality ads that provide value to users, making them less likely to use ad blockers.

- Invest in native advertising, which integrates seamlessly with the content and is less likely to be blocked.

- Focus on content marketing and other organic strategies to reach audiences.

Privacy Concerns and Regulations: Increasing concerns about data privacy and the implementation of regulations like GDPR and CCPA have made it more challenging to collect and use personal data for ad targeting.

Solution: To navigate privacy concerns, marketers should:

- Ensure compliance with all relevant data protection regulations.

- Be transparent with users about data collection practices and obtain explicit consent.

- Use first-party data and focus on building direct relationships with customers.

Measuring ROI Consistently and Accurately: Measuring the return on investment (ROI) for digital advertising can be complex due to the multitude of metrics and the difficulty in attributing sales directly to ads, especially in multi-channel campaigns.

Solution: To effectively measure ROI, marketers should:

- Use comprehensive analytics tools that provide detailed insights into ad performance across channels.

- Implement multi-touch attribution models to understand the customer journey better.

- Track key performance indicators (KPIs) that align with business goals, such as conversion rates and customer acquisition costs.

Keeping Up with Technology and New Trends: The digital advertising landscape is constantly evolving, with new technologies, platforms, and trends emerging regularly. Staying updated can be challenging.

Solution: To stay current, marketers should:

- Continuously educate themselves through industry blogs, webinars, and conferences.

- Experiment with new platforms and ad formats to understand their potential.

- Collaborate with digital marketing experts and agencies for insights and guidance.

Preventing Ad Fraud: Ad fraud, including practices like click fraud and impression fraud, can waste a significant portion of the advertising budget and skew performance metrics.

Solution: To mitigate ad fraud, marketers should:

- Use ad verification and fraud detection tools to monitor and prevent fraudulent activities.

- Choose reputable ad networks and demand transparency in reporting.

- Regularly review and analyze traffic sources and ad performance data.

Creating High-Quality Content That Will Relate To Target Audience: Producing high-quality, engaging ad content that resonates with the target audience requires creativity, time, and resources.

Solution: To ensure high-quality content, marketers should:

- Invest in skilled content creators, designers, and copywriters.

- Conduct audience research to understand preferences and pain points.

- Use A/B testing to identify the most effective ad creatives and messages.

Integration Across Channels: Managing and integrating campaigns across multiple digital channels (e.g., social media, search engines, display networks) can be complex and requires a cohesive strategy.

Solution: To achieve integration, marketers should:

- Develop a unified marketing strategy that aligns with overall business goals.

- Use marketing automation and management platforms to streamline campaign execution and tracking.

- Ensure consistent messaging and branding across all channels.

Budget Management: Allocating and managing the advertising budget effectively across various channels and campaigns can be challenging, especially with fluctuating costs and performance.

Solution: To manage budgets effectively, marketers should:

- Use data-driven approaches to allocate budgets based on past performance and potential ROI.

- Continuously monitor and adjust spending based on real-time performance metrics.

- Implement flexible budgeting strategies that allow for quick reallocation as needed.

Audience Targeting and Segmentation: Accurately targeting the right audience segments and ensuring that ads reach potential customers can be difficult, especially with changing algorithms and data limitations.

Solution: To improve targeting, marketers should:

- Leverage advanced targeting options provided by advertising platforms, such as lookalike audiences and retargeting.

- Use first-party data and CRM tools to create detailed customer profiles.

- Regularly update and refine audience segments based on performance data and market research.

Best Practice: Implement a Data-Driven Approach to Digital Advertising

Managing digital advertising effectively requires a data-driven approach that leverages analytics, precise targeting, and continuous optimization. By using data to inform your decisions, you can ensure your ads reach the right audience, maximize ROI, and adjust your strategy based on performance insights.

Steps to Implement a Data-Driven Approach to Digital Advertising

1. Define Clear Objectives and KPIs

- Business Goals: Align your digital advertising efforts with your overarching business goals (e.g., brand awareness, lead generation, sales).

- Specific Objectives: Set specific, measurable objectives for each campaign, such as increasing website traffic by 20% or generating 100 new leads.

- KPIs: Identify key performance indicators (KPIs) such as click-through rates (CTR), conversion rates, cost per click (CPC), and return on ad spend (ROAS).

2. Understand and Segment Your Audience

- Audience Research: Use tools like Google Analytics and social media insights to understand your audience's demographics, interests, and behavior.

- Segmentation: Segment your audience based on factors such as age, location, interests, and purchasing behavior to tailor your ads more effectively.

3. Choose the Right Advertising Platforms

- **Platform Selection:** Choose platforms that align with your target audience and campaign goals. Options include Google Ads, Facebook Ads, Instagram Ads, LinkedIn Ads, and more.

- **Multi-Channel Strategy:** Utilize a multi-channel strategy to reach your audience across different platforms and touchpoints.

4. Develop Compelling Ad Creative

- **Engaging Visuals:** Use high-quality images and videos that capture attention and convey your message effectively.

- **Persuasive Copy:** Write compelling ad copy that highlights the benefits of your product or service and includes a clear call-to-action (CTA).

- **A/B Testing:** Conduct A/B testing on different ad creatives to identify which elements (e.g., images, headlines, CTAs) perform best.

5. Implement Precise Targeting

- **Audience Targeting:** Use detailed targeting options available on advertising platforms to reach specific audience segments.

- **Remarketing:** Set up remarketing campaigns to re-engage users who have previously interacted with your website or ads.

- **Lookalike Audiences:** Create lookalike audiences to reach new users who share characteristics with your existing customers.

6. Set Up Conversion Tracking

- **Tracking Setup:** Implement conversion tracking using tools like Google Analytics, Facebook Pixel, and platform-specific tracking codes.

- **Attribution Models:** Use appropriate attribution models to understand which touchpoints in the customer journey contribute to conversions.

7. Monitor and Optimize Campaigns

- **Real-Time Monitoring:** Continuously monitor your campaigns to track performance and identify areas for improvement.

- **Performance Analysis:** Analyze data to understand what's working and what's not. Look at metrics such as CTR, conversion rate, and CPC.

- **Budget Allocation:** Adjust your budget allocation based on the performance of different campaigns and ad sets.

8. Conduct Regular Reporting and Analysis

- **Comprehensive Reports:** Generate regular reports that provide insights into campaign performance, ROI, and key metrics.

- **Insight Extraction:** Use these reports to extract actionable insights and inform future advertising strategies.

9. Continuously Optimize and Scale

- **Ongoing Optimization:** Continuously test and optimize your ad creatives, targeting, and bidding strategies.

- **Scaling Successful Campaigns:** Scale up successful campaigns by increasing budgets and expanding targeting while maintaining performance.

By implementing a data-driven approach to digital advertising, your business can effectively reach and engage its target audience, optimize ad spend, and achieve measurable results that contribute to overall business growth. And while digital advertising offers numerous benefits, it also presents several challenges that require careful management and strategic planning. By understanding and addressing issues such as ad fatigue, privacy concerns, ad fraud, and budget management, businesses can optimize their digital advertising efforts and achieve better results. Staying informed about industry trends, using advanced tools, and focusing on high-quality content will help marketers navigate the complexities of digital advertising and drive successful campaigns.

CHAPTER 6
The Value of Social Media Marketing

Social media marketing (SMM) refers to the use of social media platforms to promote products, services, and brands, engage with customers, and drive business goals. It encompasses a variety of activities, including content creation, community management, paid advertising, and analytics, all aimed at building a brand's online presence and fostering meaningful relationships with its audience.

Social media marketing is critical in today's digital landscape due to the widespread use of social media platforms. Here are some key reasons why SMM is important:

- Massive Audience Reach: Platforms like Facebook, Instagram, Twitter, LinkedIn, and TikTok have billions of active users, offering businesses an unparalleled opportunity to reach a large and diverse audience.

- Targeted Advertising: Social media platforms provide advanced targeting options, allowing businesses to reach specific demographics, interests, and behaviors, ensuring their ads are seen by the most relevant audience.

- Enhanced Customer Engagement: Social media allows for direct interaction with customers, enabling businesses to respond to inquiries, gather feedback, and build relationships in real time.

- Cost-Effective Marketing: Compared to traditional advertising, social media marketing can be more affordable, with flexible budgeting options and a wide range of free tools and resources.

- Brand Awareness and Loyalty: Consistent, high-quality content and engagement on social media can significantly boost brand awareness and foster customer loyalty.

- Insights and Analytics: Social media platforms offer robust analytics tools that provide valuable insights into audience behavior, campaign performance, and overall strategy effectiveness.

Now, let's look at the different components of social media marketing.

Content Creation and Sharing: Content is the backbone of social media marketing. Creating engaging, valuable, and relevant content tailored to each platform is essential for capturing the audience's attention and driving engagement.

- Types of Content:
  - o Text Posts: Short, compelling messages that prompt user interaction.
  - o Images: High-quality photos, infographics, and visually appealing memes.
  - o Videos: Engaging video content, including tutorials, behind-the-scenes footage, and live streams.
  - o Stories: Temporary content that disappears after 24 hours, perfect for behind-the-scenes glimpses and real-time updates.

- o User-Generated Content (UGC): Content created by customers, such as reviews, testimonials, and photos, which can build trust and authenticity.
- Content Strategy:
  - o Consistency: Regular posting to maintain visibility and engagement.
  - o Variety: Mixing different types of content to keep the audience engaged.
  - o Quality: Ensuring all content is high-quality, informative, and aligns with the brand's voice and values.

Community Management: Building and nurturing a community around your brand involves actively engaging with followers, responding to comments and messages, and fostering a sense of belonging.

- Engagement: Liking, commenting, and sharing user posts, and starting conversations with followers.
- Customer Service: Addressing customer inquiries and resolving issues promptly through social media channels.
- Community Building: Creating and managing groups or communities where like-minded individuals can connect and share their experiences related to your brand.

Social Media Advertising: Paid advertising on social media platforms can amplify your reach and target specific audiences to achieve marketing goals such as driving traffic, generating leads, or boosting sales.

- Ad Formats:

o Image Ads: Static visuals that highlight products or services.

o Video Ads: Engaging video content that captures the viewer's attention.

o Carousel Ads: Multiple images or videos in a single ad, allowing users to swipe through.

o Sponsored Posts: Paid promotions of regular posts to reach a wider audience.

o Stories Ads: Full-screen vertical ads that appear between user stories.

- Targeting Options:

o Demographics: Age, gender, location, education, etc.

o Interests: Hobbies, likes, and other interests.

o Behaviors: Purchase behavior, device usage, etc.

o Custom Audiences: Using existing customer data to target ads.

o Lookalike Audiences: Finding new users similar to your best existing customers.

4. Analytics and Reporting: Monitoring and analyzing social media performance is crucial for understanding what works and what doesn't and how to optimize your strategy.

- Key Metrics:

o Reach: The number of unique users who saw your content.

o Impressions: The total number of times your content was displayed.

- o Engagement: Likes, comments, shares, and other interactions.

- o Click-Through Rate (CTR): The percentage of users who clicked on a link in your post or ad.

- o Conversion Rate: The percentage of users who completed a desired action (e.g., making a purchase) after clicking on your ad.

- o Return on Investment (ROI): The financial return from your social media marketing efforts.

- Tools for Analytics:

- o Platform-Specific Analytics: Built-in tools provided by social media platforms, such as Facebook Insights, Instagram Insights, and Twitter Analytics.

- o Third-Party Tools: Comprehensive analytics tools like Hootsuite, Sprout Social, and Google Analytics.

Influencer Marketing: Collaborating with influencers can help brands reach new audiences, build credibility, and drive engagement. Influencers have established trust with their followers, making their endorsements valuable.

- Types of Influencers:

- o Mega-Influencers: Celebrities with millions of followers.

- o Macro-Influencers: Well-known individuals with hundreds of thousands of followers.

- o Micro-Influencers: Niche influencers with 10,000 to 100,000 followers.

- o Nano-Influencers: Every day, individuals with 1,000 to 10,000 followers.

- Choosing the Right Influencers:

  o Relevance: The influencer's content and audience should align with your brand.

  o Engagement: High engagement rates often indicate a loyal and active follower base.

  o Authenticity: Influencers who genuinely use and appreciate your products can provide more credible endorsements.

Social Listening: Social listening involves monitoring social media platforms for mentions of your brand, competitors, and industry-related topics. This helps gather valuable insights and inform your marketing strategy.

- Benefits of Social Listening:

  o Customer Feedback: Understanding customer sentiments and addressing concerns.

  o Competitor Analysis: Keeping an eye on competitors' activities and strategies.

  o Market Trends: Identifying emerging trends and opportunities in your industry.

  o Crisis Management: Detecting and addressing potential PR crises early.

- Tools for Social Listening:

  o Brandwatch

  o Hootsuite Insights

  o Mention

  o Sprout Social

Developing a Social Media Marketing Strategy

Creating a successful social media marketing strategy is like creating a business plan. You start with what are your goals and who you are targeting and research multiple social media websites to figure out which site has your target audience. And do they provide you with tools to communicate with your target audience. Let's dive deeper into each of the key steps:

1. Define Your Goals

Clearly outline what you want to achieve with your social media marketing efforts. Common goals include:

- Increasing brand awareness

- Driving website traffic

- Generating leads

- Boosting sales

- Improving customer engagement

- Enhancing customer loyalty

Understand Your Audience: Conduct thorough research to understand your target audience's demographics, interests, behaviors, and preferences. Use tools like Facebook Audience Insights and Twitter Analytics to gather data.

Choose the Right Platforms: Select the social media platforms that best align with your audience and business goals. Each platform has its unique features and audience demographics:

- Facebook: Broad audience, good for community building and advertising.

- Instagram: Visual content, popular among younger demographics.

- Twitter: Real-time updates, ideal for news and customer service.

- LinkedIn: Professional networking, B2B marketing.

- TikTok: Short-form video content, popular among Gen Z.

Create Engaging Content: Develop a content plan that includes a mix of content types tailored to each platform. Ensure your content is engaging, valuable, and aligned with your brand voice.

Schedule and Publish Content: Use social media management tools like Hootsuite, Buffer, or Sprout Social to schedule and publish content consistently. Consistency is key to maintaining engagement and visibility.

Engage with Your Audience: Actively engage with your audience by responding to comments, messages, and mentions. Show appreciation for positive feedback and address any concerns or questions promptly.

Monitor and Analyze Performance: Regularly monitor your social media performance using analytics tools. Track key metrics to assess the effectiveness of your strategy and identify areas for improvement.

Adjust and Optimize: Use the insights gained from your analytics to refine your strategy. Continuously test different types of content, posting times, and ad formats to optimize your social media marketing efforts.

Challenges of Social Media Marketing:

While social media marketing offers numerous benefits, it also presents several challenges:

- **Algorithm Changes:** Social media platforms frequently update their algorithms, affecting the visibility and reach of organic content. Staying updated with these changes and adapting your strategy accordingly is crucial.

- **High Competition:** The popularity of social media marketing means that businesses face high competition for audience attention. Creating unique and high-quality content that stands out is essential.

- **Managing Multiple Platforms:** Each social media platform has its unique features and best practices. Managing multiple platforms can be time-consuming and requires a tailored approach for each.

- **Measuring ROI:** Quantifying the ROI of social media marketing can be challenging due to the difficulty in attributing sales directly to social media activities. Using advanced analytics and attribution models can help.

- **Ad Fatigue:** Users may become tired of seeing the same ads repeatedly, leading to decreased engagement and effectiveness. Regularly refreshing ad creatives and targeting strategies is necessary.

Best Practice: Develop and Implement a Holistic Social Media Strategy

Managing social media marketing effectively involves creating a comprehensive strategy that integrates your business goals, audience insights, and content planning. A holistic approach ensures that all aspects of your social media presence work together to build brand awareness, engage with your audience, and drive conversions.

Steps to Develop and Implement a Holistic Social Media Strategy

1. Define Your Goals and Objectives

- **Business Alignment:** Align your social media goals with your overall business objectives (e.g., increasing brand awareness, driving website traffic, generating leads).

- **SMART Goals:** Set Specific, Measurable, Achievable, Relevant, and Time-bound goals for your social media efforts.

2. Understand Your Audience

- **Audience Research:** Use tools like Facebook Insights, Twitter Analytics, and Instagram Insights to gather data on your audience's demographics, interests, and behaviors.

- **Buyer Personas:** Develop detailed buyer personas to represent your target audience segments.

3. Conduct a Social Media Audit

- Current Presence: Review your existing social media profiles to assess their performance and identify strengths and weaknesses.

- Competitive Analysis: Analyze your competitors' social media activities to understand what's working in your industry.

4. Choose the Right Platforms

- Platform Selection: Select social media platforms that align with your target audience and business goals. Common platforms include Facebook, Instagram, Twitter, LinkedIn, Pinterest, and TikTok.

- Platform-Specific Strategies: Develop tailored strategies for each platform based on their unique features and user base.

5. Develop a Content Strategy

- Content Themes: Identify key content themes that resonate with your audience and align with your brand values.

- Content Types: Plan a mix of content types, such as blog posts, videos, infographics, stories, and user-generated content.

- Content Calendar: Create a content calendar to schedule and organize your content in advance, ensuring consistency and regular posting.

6. Create Engaging and Valuable Content

- High-Quality Visuals: Use high-quality images, videos, and graphics to make your content visually appealing.

- Compelling Copy: Write engaging captions and copy that encourage interaction and convey your brand message effectively.

- Value-Driven Content: Focus on providing value to your audience through educational, entertaining, or inspiring content.

7. Engage with Your Audience

- **Active Engagement:** Respond to comments, messages, and mentions promptly to build relationships and foster community.

- **Interactive Content:** Use polls, quizzes, live videos, and Q&A sessions to encourage audience participation.

- **User-Generated Content:** Encourage your audience to create and share content related to your brand, products, or services.

8. Leverage Paid Social Advertising

- **Ad Campaigns:** Use paid advertising options on social media platforms to amplify your reach and target specific audience segments.

- **Targeting Options:** Utilize detailed targeting options to reach users based on demographics, interests, behaviors, and lookalike audiences.

- **Performance Tracking:** Monitor the performance of your ad campaigns and adjust them based on insights and results.

9. Monitor and Analyze Performance

- **Analytics Tools:** Use social media analytics tools to track key metrics such as engagement, reach, impressions, click-through rates, and conversions.

- **Regular Reporting:** Generate regular reports to analyze your social media performance and identify trends and areas for improvement.

- Feedback Loop: Use feedback from your audience and stakeholders to refine your strategy and content.

10. Continuously Optimize and Adapt

- Ongoing Optimization: Regularly update your content strategy based on performance data and evolving audience preferences.

- Stay Updated: Keep up with the latest social media trends, platform updates, and best practices to ensure your strategy remains effective.

- Experiment and Innovate: Experiment with new content formats, posting times, and engagement tactics to discover what works best for your brand.

Future Trends in Social Media Marketing. Social media marketing is constantly evolving. Here are some trends to watch:

- **Video Content Dominance:** Video content, especially short-form videos on platforms like TikTok and Instagram Reels, is becoming increasingly popular. Brands should invest in video content creation to stay relevant.

- **Social Commerce:** Social media platforms are integrating shopping features, allowing users to purchase products directly from the platform. Social commerce is set to grow, providing new opportunities for businesses.

- **Augmented Reality (AR) and Virtual Reality (VR):** AR and VR technologies are being integrated into social media platforms, offering immersive experiences for users. Brands can leverage these technologies for interactive marketing campaigns.

- **Personalization and AI:** Artificial intelligence (AI) and machine learning are enabling more personalized and targeted advertising. Leveraging AI for social media marketing can improve targeting and engagement.

- **Increased Focus on Privacy:** With growing concerns about data privacy, social media platforms are enhancing their privacy features. Businesses must prioritize transparency and ethical data practices in their marketing efforts.

Social media marketing is a powerful tool for businesses to connect with their audience, build brand awareness, and achieve their marketing goals. By understanding the key components of social media marketing, developing a strategic approach, and staying updated with industry trends, businesses can effectively leverage social media to drive growth and success. As the digital landscape continues to evolve, staying agile and adaptable will be essential for maximizing the benefits of social media marketing.

Five Detailed Examples of How to Use Social Media for Business

Social media provides businesses with numerous opportunities to engage with their audience, promote products or services, and build brand loyalty. Here are detailed examples of how businesses can effectively use social media:

How a Coffee Company Leverages Social Media for Customer Engagement and Community Building.

Social Media Strategy:

- Coffee shops use social media platforms like Instagram, Twitter, and Facebook to engage with their customers and build a sense of community around their brand.

- Frequently post user-generated content, such as photos and stories shared by their customers enjoying coffee shop products.

- Coffee shops can also run interactive campaigns and challenges, encouraging customers to share their experiences and participate in brand-related activities.

Social Media Campaign Execution:

- Instagram: coffee shop posts high-quality images and videos showcasing their beverages, new product launches, and in-store experiences. They use hashtags like #coffeeshop to encourage customers to share their photos, which Starbucks then reposts, creating a sense of community and customer inclusion.

- Twitter: The coffee shop engages with customers by responding to tweets, addressing complaints, and acknowledging compliments. They run seasonal campaigns like the Red Cup Contest, where followers share photos of their holiday-themed cups for a chance to be featured on coffee shops' social media channels.

- Facebook: Coffee Shop uses Facebook to share longer-form content, including behind-the-scenes stories, customer testimonials, and updates on its social responsibility initiatives.

Social Media Outcome and Results:

- This strategy helps the coffee shop foster a loyal customer base by creating a two-way communication channel and making customers feel valued and connected to the brand.

How a Computer Company Leverages Social Media For Product Launches and Promotions.

Social Media Strategy:

- Computer companies use social media to create buzz and excitement around their product launches. Their strategy includes teaser campaigns, live event streaming, and detailed product showcases.

- They leverage platforms like YouTube, Twitter, and Instagram to reach a wide audience and generate anticipation for upcoming products.

Social Media Campaign Execution:

- YouTube: the computer company streams its product launch events live on YouTube, allowing millions of viewers worldwide to watch the unveiling of new products. They also post detailed product videos showcasing the features and design of new devices.

- Twitter: Computer company uses Twitter to post live updates during their events, sharing key highlights and moments with followers. They also use promoted tweets to reach a broader audience and drive traffic to their event live streams and product pages.

- Instagram: the computer company shares high-quality photos and videos of their new products, highlighting their design and features. They use Instagram Stories to provide behind-the-scenes glimpses and exclusive looks at upcoming products.

Social Media Outcome and Results:

- Computer company's social media strategy effectively generates hype and anticipation for their product launches, driving significant engagement and media coverage. This results in high demand and strong sales performance for new products.

How a Shoe and Apparel Company can Leverage Social Media For Customer Support and Service.

Social Media Strategy:

- The shoe company, an online shoe and clothing retailer, uses social media to provide exceptional customer support and service. They prioritize quick responses and personalized interactions to resolve customer issues and enhance satisfaction.

- Platforms like Twitter and Facebook are integral to their customer support strategy.

Social Media Campaign Execution:

- Twitter: The shoe company actively monitors mentions and direct messages on Twitter to address customer inquiries and resolve issues promptly. They have a dedicated customer service handle, @shoecompany_Service, where customers can reach out for support. The shoe company's customer service team responds quickly and often goes above and beyond to ensure customer satisfaction.

- Facebook: The shoe company uses Facebook to handle customer support through comments and messages. They also share helpful content, such as size guides and product care tips, to assist customers with common questions.

Social Media Outcome and Results:

- The shoe company's commitment to excellent customer service on social media has helped it build a strong reputation for customer-centricity. This approach has resulted in high customer loyalty and positive word-of-mouth marketing.

How to Leverage Social Media for Commerce and Direct Sales.

Social Media Strategy:

- A beauty and skincare brand uses social media as a primary sales channel. They leverage platforms like Instagram and Facebook to drive direct sales through shoppable posts and integrated e-commerce features.

- Their strategy focuses on showcasing products in a relatable and authentic manner, often featuring real customers and influencers.

Social Media Campaign Execution:

1. Instagram: Beauty and skincare brands use Instagram Shopping to tag products in their posts and stories, allowing users to purchase directly from the app. They share user-generated content and influencer posts to

showcase how real people use their products, adding authenticity and trust to their brand.

2. Facebook: Beauty and skincare brands run targeted ads on Facebook to promote specific products and drive traffic to their online store. They use Facebook's dynamic ads to retarget users who have shown interest in their products, offering personalized recommendations and promotions.

3. Instagram Stories: Beauty and skincare brands frequently use Instagram Stories to share product demos, tutorials, and behind-the-scenes content. They include swipe-up links in their stories, directing users to purchase pages.

Social Media Outcome and Results:

- Beauty and skincare brand commerce strategy has contributed to their rapid growth and success in the beauty industry. By making the shopping experience seamless and engaging, they drive significant sales through social media channels.

Social media marketing offers a wide array of opportunities for businesses to connect with their audience, promote their products, and build a loyal customer base. By leveraging social media for customer engagement, product launches, customer support, brand storytelling, and social commerce, businesses can achieve their marketing goals and drive growth. The key to success lies in understanding the unique strengths of each platform, creating high-quality content, and maintaining a consistent and authentic presence.

CHAPTER 7
Build a Customer Relation Management (CRM)

Customer Relationship Management (CRM) system is a technology solution that helps businesses manage and analyze interactions with current and potential customers. The primary goal of a CRM system is to improve business relationships, streamline processes, and enhance profitability. CRM systems are designed to compile information on customers across different channels—or points of contact—between the customer and the company, which could include the company's website, telephone, live chat, direct mail, marketing materials, and social media.

Now, let's understand the different components of a CRM System.

1. Contact Management: This is the core feature of any CRM system, which involves storing and managing contact information such as names, addresses, phone numbers, and email addresses. It also includes tracking interactions and communications with contacts, providing a complete view of customer history.

2. Sales Management: CRM systems help manage sales processes, track leads and opportunities, and automate various sales tasks. This includes sales forecasting, managing sales pipelines, and tracking performance against sales targets.

3. Marketing Automation: Marketing automation features enable businesses to create, execute, and analyze marketing campaigns. This includes email marketing, social media marketing, and campaign management. CRM systems can help segment customers for targeted marketing efforts and track the effectiveness of marketing campaigns.

4. Customer Service and Support: CRM systems provide tools for managing customer service activities, including ticketing systems, help desks, and customer support automation. This ensures that customer inquiries and issues are tracked and resolved efficiently.

5. Analytics and Reporting: CRM systems offer powerful analytics and reporting tools to help businesses analyze customer data, measure performance, and make data-driven decisions. This includes generating reports on sales, customer interactions, and campaign performance.

6. Workflow Automation: Workflow automation features help streamline and automate repetitive tasks and processes. This improves efficiency and ensures consistency in how customer interactions are handled.

7. Integration Capabilities: CRM systems can integrate with other business tools and systems, such as email platforms, social media networks, e-commerce systems, and more. This ensures seamless data flow and enhances the functionality of the CRM system.

Here are some benefits for a business to have a CRM System implemented:

- Improved Customer Relationships: By having a centralized database of customer information, businesses can offer more personalized and consistent interactions, leading to improved customer satisfaction and loyalty.

- Increased Efficiency: CRM systems automate many routine tasks, freeing up time for employees to focus on more strategic activities. This increases overall efficiency and productivity.

- Better Data Management: CRM systems provide a centralized repository for all customer data, ensuring that information is organized, accessible, and up-to-date. This improves data accuracy and reduces the risk of errors.

- Enhanced Communication: CRM systems facilitate better communication within teams and across departments by providing a unified view of customer interactions. This ensures that everyone is on the same page and can collaborate effectively.

- Insightful Analytics: With advanced analytics and reporting tools, businesses can gain valuable insights into customer behavior, sales trends, and campaign performance. This helps in making informed decisions and identifying opportunities for growth.

- Scalability: CRM systems are scalable and can grow with the business. As the business expands, the CRM system can be adjusted to accommodate more users, additional data, and new functionalities.

Below are examples of the most popular CRM Systems available in the market that you should investigate and determine which is best for your business.

- o **Salesforce:** Salesforce is one of the most popular CRM systems, known for its robust features and extensive customization options. It offers solutions for sales, customer service, marketing, and more, making it suitable for businesses of all sizes.

o **HubSpot CRM:** HubSpot CRM is known for its user-friendly interface and integration with HubSpot's marketing, sales, and service tools. It offers a free version with essential features, making it accessible for small businesses and startups.

o **Zoho CRM:** Zoho CRM is a cost-effective solution that offers a wide range of features, including sales automation, marketing automation, and customer support. It is known for its flexibility and integration capabilities.

o **Microsoft Dynamics 365:** Microsoft Dynamics 365 combines CRM and ERP capabilities, offering solutions for sales, customer service, field service, and more. It is highly customizable and integrates well with other Microsoft products.

o **Pipedrive:** Pipedrive is a CRM system designed with sales teams in mind. It offers a visual sales pipeline, email integration, and sales automation features, making it easy to manage and track sales activities.

A Customer Relationship Management (CRM) system is an essential tool for businesses looking to improve customer relationships, streamline processes, and drive growth. By centralizing customer data and automating various tasks, CRM systems enhance efficiency, improve communication, and provide valuable insights that help businesses make informed decisions. Whether you are a small business or a large enterprise, investing in a CRM system can significantly impact your ability to attract, retain, and satisfy customers.

Here are examples of CRM system usage across multiple businesses. This can help you envision how you can use a CRM System for your business.

A PRACTICAL GUIDE TO DIGITAL MARKETING

Customer Relationship Management (CRM) systems play a crucial role in business by enabling businesses to manage and analyze customer interactions, streamline processes, and enhance relationship-building efforts. Here are three detailed examples of CRM usage:

Implement a CRM System to Manage Sales Leads

A Software-as-a-Service (SaaS) Company

- **Lead Capture and Segmentation:** The SaaS company uses a CRM system to capture leads from various sources, such as website forms, webinars, trade shows, and email campaigns. The CRM automatically segments these leads based on criteria such as industry, company size, job title, and lead source.

- **Lead Scoring:** The CRM system assigns scores to leads based on their engagement levels, such as website visits, content downloads, and email interactions. This helps prioritize leads that are more likely to convert.

- **Automated Nurturing Campaigns:** The company uses CRM to set up automated email nurturing campaigns tailored to each segment. For example, leads from the financial industry receive content related to financial technology trends and case studies. These campaigns include a series of emails that educate and guide leads through the sales funnel.

Key Benefits:

- Increased efficiency in lead management and nurturing.

- Improved lead segmentation and targeting.
- Higher conversion rates due to personalized and relevant content.

A Manufacturing Equipment Supplier

- **Account Targeting:** The CRM system helps the supplier identify and prioritize high-value accounts based on criteria such as revenue potential, strategic fit, and past purchase history. The marketing team collaborates with the sales team to define target accounts and develop tailored strategies for each.

- **Personalized Campaigns:** Using CRM data, the supplier creates highly personalized marketing campaigns for each target account. This includes customized content, personalized emails, and targeted ads. For instance, a campaign for a large automotive manufacturer might focus on specific equipment solutions relevant to their production processes.

- **Tracking and Analytics:** The CRM tracks the engagement and interactions of each target account with the campaigns. This includes email opens, website visits, and content downloads. The marketing team uses this data to refine their strategies and tailor follow-up actions.

Key Benefits:

- Enhanced alignment between marketing and sales teams.

- More effective targeting of high-value accounts.
- Improved engagement and conversion rates with personalized marketing efforts.

An IT Services Provider

- Customer Insights: The CRM system provides a 360-degree view of each customer, including past interactions, purchase history, and service usage. This information helps the IT services provider understand customer needs and preferences.

- Retention Campaigns: The marketing team uses the CRM to identify customers at risk of churn based on engagement metrics and service usage patterns. They launch targeted retention campaigns that include personalized emails, special offers, and proactive support outreach.

- Upselling and Cross-Selling: The CRM system identifies opportunities for upselling and cross-selling based on customer data. For example, if a customer is using a basic IT support package, the CRM can highlight the potential benefits of upgrading to a premium support package or adding additional services like cybersecurity solutions. The marketing team then creates personalized upselling campaigns to promote these offerings.

Key Benefits:

- Improved customer retention through proactive engagement and support.

- Increased revenue from upselling and cross-selling initiatives.

- Enhanced customer satisfaction and loyalty.

How To Implement a CRM System:

- Implementing a CRM system successfully requires careful planning, cross-functional collaboration, and ongoing commitment. By following these steps, businesses can ensure a smooth CRM implementation that enhances customer relationships, streamlines processes and drives growth. The key to success lies in defining clear objectives, choosing the right CRM solution, training users effectively, and continuously optimizing the system to meet evolving business needs.

- Implementing a Customer Relationship Management (CRM) system is a strategic process that involves several critical steps to ensure its success. Here's a detailed guide to help you implement a CRM system effectively:

Identify Business Needs

- Understand the specific needs and challenges your business faces in managing customer relationships.

- Define clear goals and objectives for the CRM implementation, such as improving sales processes, enhancing customer service, or increasing marketing effectiveness.

Set Measurable Goals

- Establish key performance indicators (KPIs) to measure the success of the CRM implementation.

- Examples of KPIs include customer satisfaction scores, lead conversion rates, sales cycle length, and customer retention rates.

Form a Cross-Functional Team

- Include representatives from various departments such as sales, marketing, customer service, IT, and finance.

- Ensure the team has a mix of strategic and technical skills to handle different aspects of the CRM implementation.

Assign Roles and Responsibilities

- Define clear roles and responsibilities for each team member.

- Appoint a project manager to oversee the implementation process and ensure timely completion of tasks.

Evaluate CRM Options

- Research and evaluate different CRM solutions based on your business needs and budget.

- Consider factors such as features, scalability, ease of use, integration capabilities, and customer support.

Conduct Demos and Trials

- Request product demonstrations and trial versions from CRM vendors.

- Involve end-users in the evaluation process to gather feedback and ensure the chosen CRM meets their needs.

Select the CRM Vendor

- Choose a CRM vendor that aligns with your business goals and offers the necessary support and training.

- Negotiate terms, pricing, and implementation support with the vendor.

Best Practice: Implementing a Customer Relationship Management (CRM) System for Your Business

A Customer Relationship Management (CRM) system is essential for managing interactions with current and potential customers, improving customer service, and driving sales growth. Implementing a CRM system effectively requires careful planning, clear objectives, and ongoing management. Here's a step-by-step best practice guide to building a successful CRM system for your business:

1. Define Your CRM Objectives

- **Business Goals:** Align your CRM objectives with your overall business goals, such as increasing sales, improving customer satisfaction, and enhancing customer retention.

- **Specific Objectives:** Set clear, measurable objectives for your CRM system, such as reducing customer response times, increasing lead conversion rates, or improving the accuracy of sales forecasting.

2. Choose the Right CRM Platform

- **Platform Selection:** Choose a CRM platform that fits your business needs, size, and budget. Popular options include Salesforce, HubSpot, Zoho CRM, and Microsoft Dynamics 365.

- **Feature Assessment:** Evaluate the features of different CRM platforms, such as contact management, sales automation, marketing automation, customer service, and analytics.

- **Scalability:** Ensure the CRM platform can scale with your business as it grows and can integrate with other tools and systems you use.

3. Involve Key Stakeholders

- **Cross-Functional Team:** Form a cross-functional team that includes representatives from sales, marketing, customer service, and IT to ensure all perspectives and needs are considered.

- **Stakeholder Buy-In:** Involve key stakeholders in the decision-making process to ensure buy-in and support for the CRM implementation.

4. Map Your Customer Journey

- **Customer Touchpoints:** Identify all customer touchpoints, from initial contact to post-purchase support, and map out the customer journey.

- **Process Alignment:** Align your CRM processes with the customer journey to ensure a seamless and consistent customer experience.

5. Customize the CRM System

- **Tailored Workflows:** Customize the CRM workflows to match your business processes, including lead management, sales pipeline stages, and customer support processes.

- **Custom Fields:** Create custom fields and data structures to capture all relevant customer information and ensure it aligns with your specific needs.

6. Data Migration and Integration

- **Data Clean-Up:** Clean and organize your existing customer data before migrating it to the new CRM system.

- **Data Migration:** Ensure a smooth data migration process by testing and validating the data transfer.

- **System Integration:** Integrate the CRM with other systems you use, such as email marketing tools, e-commerce platforms, and accounting software, to ensure seamless data flow and functionality.

7. Train Your Team

- **Comprehensive Training:** Provide comprehensive training to all users to ensure they understand how to use the CRM system effectively.

- **Ongoing Support:** Offer ongoing support and resources, such as user guides, webinars, and a helpdesk, to address any questions or issues that arise.

8. Implement and Monitor

- **Phased Implementation:** Roll out the CRM system in phases to manage the transition smoothly and address any issues early on.

- **Monitor Usage:** Monitor how the CRM is being used and ensure that all team members are following the established processes and workflows.

- **Feedback Loop:** Collect feedback from users to identify any pain points or areas for improvement.

9. Analyze and Optimize

- **Performance Metrics:** Track key performance metrics, such as sales cycle length, lead conversion rate, and customer satisfaction, to measure the effectiveness of the CRM system.

- **Continuous Improvement:** Regularly review and analyze CRM data to identify trends, opportunities, and areas for improvement.

- **System Updates:** Keep the CRM system up-to-date with the latest features and integrations to ensure it continues to meet your business needs.

Example Business: B2B Software Company

1. Define Your CRM Objectives

- **Business Goals:** Improve lead management and increase sales by 20% over the next year.

- **Specific Objectives:** Reduce lead response time to under 24 hours and improve lead conversion rate by 15%.

2. Choose the Right CRM Platform

- **Platform Selection:** Choose Salesforce for its robust features, scalability, and strong integration capabilities.

- **Feature Assessment:** Evaluate features like lead management, sales pipeline tracking, marketing automation, and customer support.

3. Involve Key Stakeholders

- **Cross-Functional Team:** Include representatives from sales, marketing, customer support, and IT.

- **Stakeholder Buy-In:** Conduct workshops to gather input and ensure all departments are aligned with the CRM implementation plan.

4. Map Your Customer Journey

- **Customer Touchpoints:** Identify touchpoints such as initial inquiry, product demo, purchase, and post-purchase support.

- **Process Alignment:** Ensure CRM workflows align with the customer journey, including automated follow-ups and support ticket tracking.

5. Customize the CRM System

- **Tailored Workflows:** Customize workflows for lead nurturing, sales pipeline stages, and customer support processes.

- **Custom Fields:** Create custom fields to capture industry-specific data and customer preferences.

6. Data Migration and Integration

- **Data Clean-Up:** Clean and organize existing customer and lead data.

- **Data Migration:** Test and validate data migration to ensure accuracy.

- **System Integration:** Integrate Salesforce with the company's email marketing tool and accounting software.

7. Train Your Team

- **Comprehensive Training:** Conduct training sessions for all users, including sales, marketing, and support teams.

- **Ongoing Support:** Provide resources like user guides and a dedicated helpdesk.

8. Implement and Monitor

- **Phased Implementation:** Roll out the CRM system in phases, starting with the sales team.

- **Monitor Usage:** Track CRM usage and adherence to new processes.

- **Feedback Loop:** Collect feedback from users to address any issues.

9. Analyze and Optimize

- **Performance Metrics:** Track metrics like lead response time, conversion rate, and customer satisfaction.

- **Continuous Improvement:** Regularly review CRM data to identify trends and areas for improvement.

- **System Updates:** Stay current with Salesforce updates and new features.

Conclusion

By following these best practices, your business can successfully implement a CRM system that enhances customer relationships, improves sales processes, and drives business growth. A well-implemented CRM system provides a centralized platform for managing customer interactions, enabling your team to deliver personalized and efficient service while gaining valuable insights into customer behavior and preferences.

CHAPTER 8
Promote With Email Marketing Program

Email marketing is a digital marketing strategy that involves sending emails to prospects and customers to promote products, services, or content. It is one of the most effective and direct forms of communication with potential and existing customers, enabling businesses to build relationships, boost sales, and enhance customer loyalty.

Email marketing is a powerful and versatile tool that can help businesses connect with their audience, drive sales, and build lasting relationships. Let's consider some benefits or reasons for using emails to promote and grow your business.

Cost-Effective: Email marketing is one of the most cost-effective marketing strategies, offering a high return on investment (ROI). It requires minimal costs compared to traditional marketing channels.

Direct and Targeted Communication: Email allows businesses to communicate directly with their audience and deliver personalized messages to specific segments, resulting in more relevant and effective communication.

Measurable Results: Email marketing provides measurable results, allowing businesses to track and analyze the performance of their campaigns in real-time. This helps in understanding what works and what needs improvement.

High Engagement: Well-crafted emails can achieve high engagement rates, driving recipients to take desired actions such as making a purchase, signing up for an event, or visiting a website.

Customer Retention: Regular email communication helps maintain and strengthen relationships with existing customers, encouraging repeat business and fostering loyalty.

Here are a few examples of how to use email marketing for your business and create weekly communication vehicles and campaigns.

Welcome Emails: To greet new subscribers, introduce the brand, and set expectations for future communications. It's a warm welcome message, an overview of the brand or products, and an incentive such as a discount code for their first purchase.

Newsletter Emails: To keep subscribers informed about company news, updates, and valuable content. The newsletter can contain a mix of articles, blog posts, company news, upcoming events, and curated content relevant to the audience's interests.

Promotional Emails: To promote special offers, sales, new product launches, or limited-time discounts. The email should have attention-grabbing subject lines, attractive visuals, clear descriptions of the offers, and strong calls-to-action (CTAs) urging recipients to take advantage of the promotion.

Abandoned Cart Emails: If you are running an ecommerce site. Use this email to remind customers who have added products to their cart but have not completed the purchase. A reminder of the items left in the cart, often including images, product details, and a compelling CTA. Sometimes, additional incentives like discounts or free shipping are offered to encourage the completion of the purchase.

Re-Engagement Emails: To re-engage inactive subscribers who have not interacted with previous emails for a certain period. Special offers, surveys asking for feedback, or a simple message asking if they still want to receive emails. These emails aim to rekindle interest and encourage subscribers to re-engage with the brand.

Email marketing is a powerful and versatile tool that can help businesses connect with their audience, drive sales, and build lasting relationships. By focusing on building a quality email list, segmenting and personalizing content, automating workflows, and continuously analyzing performance, businesses can maximize the effectiveness of their email marketing efforts.

Best Practice: Building an Effective Email Marketing Program for Your Business

Creating an effective email marketing program involves strategic planning, audience segmentation, compelling content creation, and continuous optimization. Here's a step-by-step best practice guide to building a successful email marketing program:

1. Define Your Objectives and Goals

- Business Alignment: Align your email marketing objectives with your overall business goals, such as increasing sales, nurturing leads, or enhancing customer loyalty.

- SMART Goals: Set Specific, Measurable, Achievable, Relevant, and Time-bound goals for your email marketing efforts.

2. Build a Quality Email List

- Opt-In Forms: Use opt-in forms on your website, blog, and social media channels to collect email addresses from interested visitors.

- Lead Magnets: Offer valuable incentives, such as eBooks, webinars, or discount codes, to encourage sign-ups.

- Permission-Based: Ensure your email list is permission-based, meaning subscribers have explicitly agreed to receive emails from you.

3. Segment Your Audience

- Demographic Segmentation: Segment your email list based on demographics such as age, gender, location, and income level.

- Behavioral Segmentation: Segment based on behavior, such as past purchases, email engagement, and website activity.

- Psychographic Segmentation: Segment by interests, values, and lifestyle to create more personalized and relevant content.

4. Choose the Right Email Marketing Platform

- Platform Selection: Select an email marketing platform that fits your business needs, budget, and technical requirements. Popular options include Mailchimp, Constant Contact, HubSpot, and Campaign Monitor.

- Features Assessment: Evaluate the features offered by each platform, such as automation, segmentation, analytics, and integration capabilities.

5. Develop a Content Strategy

- Content Themes: Identify key content themes that resonate with your audience and align with your brand message.

- Content Types: Plan a mix of content types, including newsletters, promotional emails, educational content, and customer stories.

- Content Calendar: Create a content calendar to schedule and organize your email campaigns, ensuring consistency and regularity.

6. Craft Compelling Email Content

- Subject Lines: Write attention-grabbing subject lines that entice recipients to open your emails.

- Personalization: Use personalization techniques, such as addressing recipients by their first name and tailoring content based on their interests and behavior.

- Clear and Concise Copy: Ensure your email copy is clear, concise, and focused on providing value to the recipient.

- Strong CTAs: Include strong calls-to-action (CTAs) that encourage recipients to take the desired action, such as making a purchase, downloading a resource, or registering for an event.

7. Design Responsive and Engaging Emails

- Responsive Design: Ensure your emails are mobile-friendly and display correctly on all devices and screen sizes.

- Visual Appeal: Use high-quality images, graphics, and a clean layout to make your emails visually appealing.

- Interactive Elements: Incorporate interactive elements, such as buttons, videos, and surveys, to engage your audience.

8. Automate Your Email Campaigns

- Automation Workflows: Set up automation workflows for welcome emails, abandoned cart reminders, post-purchase follow-ups, and re-engagement campaigns.

- Triggered Emails: Use triggers based on user behavior or specific actions, such as clicking a link or completing a purchase, to send timely and relevant emails.

9. Monitor and Analyze Performance

- Key Metrics: Track key email marketing metrics, such as open rates, click-through rates (CTR), conversion rates, bounce rates, and unsubscribe rates.

- A/B Testing: Conduct A/B testing on subject lines, email copy, images, and CTAs to determine what works best.

- Analytics Tools: Use analytics tools provided by your email marketing platform to gain insights into your email performance and audience behavior.

10. Optimize and Refine Your Strategy

- Continuous Improvement: Regularly review your email marketing performance and identify areas for improvement.

- Feedback Loop: Gather feedback from your audience through surveys and direct responses to understand their preferences and needs.

- Stay Updated: Keep up with the latest email marketing trends, best practices, and platform updates to ensure your strategy remains effective.

Example of Email Marketing Program For an E-commerce Clothing Store

1. Define Your Objectives and Goals

- Business Goals: Increase online sales and enhance customer loyalty.

- SMART Goals: Achieve a 15% increase in email-driven sales and a 10% reduction in cart abandonment rates within six months.

2. Build a Quality Email List

- Opt-In Forms: Place opt-in forms on the homepage, blog, and product pages.

- Lead Magnets: Offer a 10% discount on the first purchase for new subscribers.

- Permission-Based: Ensure all subscribers have opted in to receive promotional emails.

3. Segment Your Audience

- Demographic Segmentation: Segment by age, gender, and location to send targeted promotions.

- Behavioral Segmentation: Segment based on past purchase history and browsing behavior.

- Psychographic Segmentation: Segment by fashion preferences and lifestyle interests.

4. Choose the Right Email Marketing Platform

- Platform Selection: Choose Mailchimp for its robust features and ease of use.

- Features Assessment: Utilize Mailchimp's automation, segmentation, and analytics capabilities.

5. Develop a Content Strategy

- Content Themes: Focus on new arrivals, seasonal promotions, fashion tips, and customer stories.

- Content Types: Include newsletters, promotional emails, and educational content.

- Content Calendar: Schedule emails to be sent bi-weekly, with additional emails for special promotions.

6. Craft Compelling Email Content

- Subject Lines: Use subject lines like "New Summer Collection Just Arrived!" or "Exclusive 20% Off for Loyal Customers!"

- Personalization: Personalize emails with the recipient's name and tailor content based on their purchase history.

- Clear and Concise Copy: Highlight key benefits and promotions clearly and concisely.

- Strong CTAs: Use CTAs like "Shop Now," "Get Your Discount," and "Discover More."

7. Design Responsive and Engaging Emails

- Responsive Design: Ensure emails are optimized for mobile devices.

- Visual Appeal: Use high-quality images of clothing items and a clean layout.

- Interactive Elements: Include clickable buttons and links to product pages.

8. Automate Your Email Campaigns

- Automation Workflows: Set up workflows for welcome emails, abandoned cart reminders, and post-purchase follow-ups.

- Triggered Emails: Send emails triggered by actions like adding items to the cart or making a purchase.

9. Monitor and Analyze Performance

- Key Metrics: Track open rates, CTR, conversion rates, and unsubscribe rates.

- A/B Testing: Test different subject lines, email designs, and CTAs.

- Analytics Tools: Use Mailchimp's analytics to gain insights into email performance.

10. Optimize and Refine Your Strategy

- Continuous Improvement: Regularly review performance and optimize email content and strategy.

- Feedback Loop: Use customer surveys to gather feedback and improve email relevance.

- Stay Updated: Keep up with the latest email marketing trends and best practices.

By following these best practices, your business can build a successful email marketing program that engages your audience, drives conversions, and supports your overall marketing goals. A well-implemented email marketing strategy provides a direct and effective way to communicate with your customers, nurture relationships, and promote your products or services.

Email Tools Needed for a Successful Email Marketing Program

Implementing a successful email marketing program requires the right set of tools to ensure that emails are effectively created, delivered, and analyzed. Here are a few email tools needed for a successful email marketing program:

Email marketing platforms are the backbone of any email marketing program, providing a comprehensive solution for creating, sending, and managing email campaigns. These platforms offer a range of features, including list management, email design, automation, and analytics.

Examples of email platforms available today:

Mailchimp:

- Offers a user-friendly interface with drag-and-drop email builders.

- Provides extensive automation features, segmentation options, and detailed analytics.

- Integrates with various other marketing and e-commerce tools.

Constant Contact:

- Known for its ease of use and robust support.

- Features include email templates, list segmentation, and reporting tools.

- Ideal for small to medium-sized businesses.

Email automation tools allow businesses to set up automated email sequences based on specific triggers or actions taken by subscribers. Automation is crucial for personalizing communication and ensuring timely delivery of emails.

Examples of automation tools:

ActiveCampaign:

- Offers advanced automation features with a visual automation builder.

- Enables complex workflows for lead nurturing, customer onboarding, and more.

- Provides extensive integration options with CRM systems and other tools.

Drip:

- Focuses on e-commerce businesses with sophisticated automation capabilities.

- Allows for behavior-based automation, personalized content, and targeted campaigns.

- Includes robust analytics and reporting features.

Email design tools help in creating visually appealing and responsive email templates that look great on any device. These tools often come with drag-and-drop editors, pre-designed templates, and customization options.

Examples of tools to help design and create the look and feel of the email content:

Canva:

- While primarily a graphic design tool, Canva offers templates specifically for email design.

- Users can create customized graphics and import them into their email marketing platform.

- Offers a wide range of design elements and templates.

BEE Free:

- Provides a user-friendly drag-and-drop email editor with various templates.

- Integrates with several email marketing platforms.

- Allows for easy creation of responsive email designs.

Analytics and reporting tools are essential for tracking the performance of email campaigns. These tools provide insights into key metrics such as open rates, click-through rates, conversions, and subscriber behavior.

Examples of tools to implement to track the effectiveness of the email marketing campaigns:

Google Analytics:

- While not exclusively for email, Google Analytics can track the performance of email campaigns through UTM parameters.

- Provides detailed insights into how email traffic interacts with your website.

- Helps in measuring the overall effectiveness of email campaigns in driving conversions.

Litmus:

- Specializes in email analytics, providing in-depth analysis of email performance.

- Includes tools for previewing emails across different devices and email clients.

- Offers features for testing subject lines, spam filters, and rendering.

CRM (Customer Relationship Management) and integration tools enable seamless data flow between your email marketing platform and other business systems. Integrating email marketing with CRM systems helps in better targeting, personalization, and tracking of customer interactions.

Examples of popular CRM systems to consider:

Salesforce:

- A leading CRM platform that integrates with various email marketing tools.

- Allows for comprehensive tracking of customer interactions and personalized email campaigns.

- Provides robust reporting and analytics features.

Zapier:

- An automation tool that connects different apps and services.

- Enables integration between email marketing platforms and other tools such as CRMs, social media, and e-commerce platforms.

- Helps automate workflows by triggering actions across different platforms.

A successful email marketing program relies on a combination of tools that facilitate the creation, automation, analysis, and integration of email campaigns. By leveraging powerful email marketing platforms, automation tools, design tools, analytics tools, and CRM integration, businesses can create effective and personalized email marketing strategies that drive engagement, nurture leads, and ultimately increase conversions.

Top of Form

Bottom of Form

CHAPTER 9
Engaging Customers With Mobile Marketing Program

Mobile marketing refers to any marketing activity that is conducted through mobile devices, such as smartphones and tablets. This can include a variety of channels and strategies designed to reach users on their mobile devices, where they spend a significant amount of their time. Mobile marketing leverages the unique capabilities of mobile devices, such as location services, push notifications, and mobile apps, to deliver highly targeted and personalized content to consumers.

Let's understand the different components that are involved in mobile marketing so that you can determine which of them we want to consider and implement in your digital marketing efforts.

SMS Marketing: This involves sending text messages to a list of subscribers who have opted in to receive updates, promotions, or alerts from a business. SMS messages are typically short and can include links to more detailed content.

MMS Marketing: Similar to SMS but allows for the inclusion of multimedia content such as images, videos, and audio clips. MMS messages are used to create more engaging and visually appealing marketing messages.

App Store Optimization (ASO): The process of optimizing mobile apps to rank higher in an app store's search results. This involves keyword optimization, creating compelling app descriptions, and encouraging positive user reviews.

In-App Advertising: Running ads within other mobile apps. These can be display ads, video ads, or interactive ads that encourage users to engage with the advertiser's content.

Push Notifications: Messages sent directly to a user's mobile device from an app they have installed. Push notifications can be used to send reminders, updates, promotional offers, or personalized messages based on user behavior.

Mobile Responsive Web Design: Ensuring that a website is optimized for mobile devices. This means the site should be easy to navigate, load quickly, and provide a seamless user experience on smaller screens.

Mobile SEO: Optimizing a website's content and structure to improve its ranking in mobile search engine results. This includes using mobile-friendly keywords, optimizing page load times, and ensuring the site is responsive.

Banner Ads: Small ads that appear at the top or bottom of the app interface. They are often used to promote app downloads or direct users to a website.

Interstitial Ads: Full-screen ads that appear at natural transition points in the app, such as between game levels or while loading a new page. These ads can be more engaging but should be used sparingly to avoid disrupting the user experience.

Native Ads: Ads that are integrated into the app's content and design, making them appear more natural and less intrusive. These ads often provide a better user experience and higher engagement rates.

Push Notifications and Personalized Messages: Sending personalized messages based on user behavior, preferences, or location. For example, a retail app might send a push notification with a discount offer when a user is near a store.

Behavioral Triggers: Sending notifications based on specific actions taken by the user within the app. For example, a fitness app might send a reminder to log a workout if the user hasn't logged in a few days.

Location-Based Marketing and Geofencing: Creating a virtual boundary around a specific location. When a user with a mobile device enters this area, they can receive targeted messages or offers. Retailers often use this to attract nearby customers.

Beacons: Small devices placed in physical locations that use Bluetooth technology to send signals to nearby mobile devices. Beacons can trigger notifications, personalized messages, or app interactions when a user is in close proximity.

Using Quick Response (QR) Codes: Two-dimensional barcodes that can be scanned using a smartphone camera to access information or websites quickly. QR codes can be used in various marketing materials to direct users to landing pages, app downloads, or promotional content.

8. Mobile Wallet Marketing: Digital wallets, such as Apple Wallet or Google Wallet, that store payment information, loyalty cards, and coupons. Businesses can send offers, discounts, and updates directly to a user's mobile wallet.

Mobile Payments: Allowing users to make purchases directly from their mobile devices using stored payment information. This can streamline the buying process and enhance the user experience.

Importance of Mobile Marketing and why you should consider it for your marketing efforts.

- **Wide Reach:** With the increasing use of mobile devices, mobile marketing allows businesses to reach a broad audience anytime and anywhere.

- **Personalization:** Mobile marketing enables highly targeted and personalized campaigns based on user behavior, preferences, and location.

- **Immediate Communication:** Mobile marketing channels, such as SMS and push notifications, allow for instant communication with customers, ensuring the timely delivery of messages and offers.

- **Higher Engagement:** Mobile devices facilitate interactive and engaging marketing experiences, such as in-app ads, mobile games, and augmented reality.

- **Data-Driven Insights:** Mobile marketing provides valuable data and insights into user behavior, helping businesses optimize their campaigns and improve ROI.

Mobile marketing is a versatile and powerful strategy that allows businesses to connect with consumers on their most frequently used devices. By leveraging various mobile marketing channels and techniques, businesses can deliver personalized, timely, and engaging content that drives customer engagement, increases conversions, and fosters brand loyalty.

Examples of Mobile Marketing Campaigns: Mobile marketing campaigns are versatile and can be tailored to fit the unique goals and audience of a business. Here are some detailed examples of successful mobile marketing campaigns across different industries:

Retail: Location-Based Push Notifications

Campaign Overview: A major retail chain implemented a location-based marketing campaign to drive foot traffic to its stores.

Strategy:

- **Geofencing:** The retailer set up geofences around its store locations. When customers with the store's app entered these geofenced areas, they received push notifications about special offers and discounts available in-store.

- **Personalization:** Notifications were personalized based on the customer's shopping history and preferences, making the offers more relevant and enticing.

- **Timing:** Notifications were sent during peak shopping hours to maximize foot traffic.

Results:

- Increased in-store visits and sales during the campaign period.

- Higher engagement rates with personalized notifications compared to generic messages.

- Improved customer satisfaction due to relevant and timely offers.

Hospitality: Mobile App Loyalty Program

Campaign Overview: A leading hotel chain launched a mobile app loyalty program to enhance customer retention and repeat bookings.

Strategy:

- **Mobile App Development:** The hotel chain developed a mobile app that allowed customers to book rooms, manage reservations, and access exclusive loyalty program benefits.

- **Push Notifications:** Customers received push notifications about special promotions, discounts, and reward points balances.

- **In-App Rewards:** The app featured a digital rewards system where customers could earn points for each booking and redeem them for free nights, upgrades, and other perks.

Results:

- Significant increase in app downloads and active users.

- Higher customer retention rates and repeat bookings.

- Enhanced customer engagement with the brand through personalized offers and rewards.

E-commerce: SMS Marketing for Flash Sales

Campaign Overview: An online fashion retailer used SMS marketing to promote flash sales and limited-time offers.

Strategy:

- **Opt-In Campaign:** The retailer encouraged customers to opt-in to receive SMS alerts by offering a discount on their first purchase.

- **Timed SMS Blasts:** During flash sales, the retailer sends SMS messages to subscribers with details about the sale and direct links to the shop.

- **Urgency and Scarcity:** Messages highlighted the limited-time nature of the offers to create a sense of urgency and drive quick conversions.

Results:

- High open and click-through rates for SMS messages.

- Significant spike in website traffic and sales during flash sales.

- Increased customer loyalty and repeat purchases from SMS subscribers.

Food & Beverage: Mobile Wallet Coupons

Campaign Overview: A popular fast-food chain used mobile wallet coupons to attract customers and boost sales.

Strategy:

- **Mobile Wallet Integration:** The chain integrated mobile wallet capabilities into its marketing strategy, allowing customers to save digital coupons in their mobile wallets.

- **Targeted Promotions:** Coupons were sent via SMS, email, and push notifications to targeted customer segments based on their location and purchase history.

- **In-Store Redemption:** Customers could easily redeem the coupons by scanning them at the point of sale, streamlining the redemption process.

Results:

- Increased coupon redemption rates compared to traditional paper coupons.

- Higher customer engagement and satisfaction due to the convenience of mobile wallet coupons.

- Boosted in-store traffic and sales during the campaign period.

Automotive: In-App Messaging for Test Drive Scheduling

Campaign Overview: A leading car manufacturer used in-app messaging to schedule test drives and follow up with potential customers.

Strategy:

- **App Features:** The manufacturer's mobile app included features for browsing car models, scheduling test drives, and accessing exclusive content.

- **Personalized In-App Messages:** Potential customers received personalized in-app messages inviting them to schedule a test drive based on their browsing behavior and preferences.

- **Follow-Up Notifications:** After the test drive, customers received follow-up notifications with special offers and financing options.

Results:

- Higher test drive bookings and showroom visits.

- Improved customer experience with personalized communication.

- Increased sales conversions from app users who scheduled test drives.

These examples demonstrate the diverse and effective ways businesses can use mobile marketing to engage customers, drive sales, and enhance brand loyalty. By leveraging various mobile marketing strategies such as location-based push notifications, mobile app loyalty programs, SMS marketing, mobile wallet coupons, and in-app messaging, businesses can create targeted and impactful campaigns that resonate with their audience and achieve their marketing objectives.

Best Practice: Building an Effective Mobile Marketing Program for Your Business

A successful mobile marketing program leverages the ubiquity of smartphones and mobile devices to engage with customers effectively. Here's a step-by-step best practice guide to building a mobile marketing program for your business:

Steps to Build a Mobile Marketing Program

1. Define Your Objectives and Goals

- **Business Alignment:** Align your mobile marketing objectives with your overall business goals, such as increasing brand awareness, driving sales, or enhancing customer engagement.

- **SMART Goals:** Set Specific, Measurable, Achievable, Relevant, and Time-bound goals for your mobile marketing efforts.

2. Understand Your Audience

- **Demographic Analysis:** Analyze the demographics of your mobile audience, such as age, gender, location, and device usage.

- **Behavioral Insights:** Understand how your audience uses their mobile devices, including app usage, browsing habits, and purchasing behavior.

- **Preferences and Needs:** Gather data on your audience's preferences and needs to tailor your mobile marketing efforts.

3. Choose the Right Mobile Marketing Channels

- Mobile Apps: Develop a mobile app to offer a personalized and engaging user experience.

- Mobile-Optimized Website: Ensure your website is mobile-friendly and provides a seamless user experience on all devices.

- SMS Marketing: Use SMS marketing to send timely and relevant messages to your audience.

- Push Notifications: Utilize push notifications to engage app users with updates, offers, and personalized messages.

- In-App Advertising: Place ads within other mobile apps to reach a broader audience.

4. Develop a Mobile Content Strategy

- Content Types: Plan a mix of content types, such as videos, articles, infographics, and interactive content, that resonate with mobile users.

- Content Frequency: Determine the optimal frequency for delivering content to avoid overwhelming your audience.

- Content Calendar: Create a content calendar to schedule and organize your mobile marketing campaigns, ensuring consistency and regularity.

5. Design Mobile-Friendly Content

- Responsive Design: Ensure all content is responsive and optimized for various screen sizes and devices.

- Visual Appeal: Use high-quality visuals and a clean layout to make your content visually appealing.

- Short and Engaging: Keep your content concise and engaging, as mobile users typically have shorter attention spans.

6. Implement Mobile SEO

- Mobile-Friendly Website: Optimize your website for mobile devices, ensuring fast load times and easy navigation.

- Local SEO: Implement local SEO strategies to target mobile users searching for businesses in their vicinity.

- Voice Search Optimization: Optimize your content for voice search, as more users are using voice commands on their mobile devices.

7. Personalize the User Experience

- User Data: Use data such as past behavior, preferences, and location to personalize the user experience.

- Dynamic Content: Deliver dynamic content that changes based on user behavior and preferences.

- Segmentation: Segment your audience to deliver more targeted and relevant messages.

8. Utilize Mobile Analytics

- Tracking and Measurement: Use mobile analytics tools to track key metrics such as app downloads, user engagement, conversion rates, and retention rates.

- User Feedback: Gather user feedback through surveys, reviews, and ratings to understand their needs and improve your mobile marketing efforts.

- A/B Testing: Conduct A/B testing on different elements of your mobile marketing campaigns to determine what works best.

9. Integrate with Other Marketing Channels

- Cross-Channel Integration: Integrate your mobile marketing efforts with other channels such as email, social media, and web to create a cohesive marketing strategy.

- Consistent Messaging: Ensure consistent messaging across all channels to reinforce your brand and marketing goals.

- Unified Customer View: Use a unified customer view to track interactions across different channels and deliver a seamless experience.

10. Monitor and Optimize

- Performance Metrics: Continuously monitor key performance metrics to measure the success of your mobile marketing campaigns.

- Optimization: Regularly optimize your campaigns based on performance data and user feedback.

- Stay Updated: Keep up with the latest mobile marketing trends, tools, and best practices to ensure your strategy remains effective.

Example Implementation

Example Business: Online Retailer

1. Define Your Objectives and Goals

- **Business Goals:** Increase mobile sales and enhance customer engagement.

- **SMART Goals:** Achieve a 20% increase in mobile-driven sales and a 15% improvement in-App user retention within six months.

2. Understand Your Audience

- Demographic Analysis: Analyze the demographics of mobile users, focusing on age, gender, and location.

- Behavioral Insights: Understand browsing habits, app usage, and purchasing behavior of mobile users.

- Preferences and Needs: Gather data on preferences for product recommendations and personalized offers.

3. Choose the Right Mobile Marketing Channels

- Mobile Apps: Develop a mobile app to offer a personalized shopping experience.

- Mobile-Optimized Website: Ensure the website is optimized for mobile with fast load times and easy navigation.

- SMS Marketing: Use SMS marketing to send promotional messages and order updates.

- Push Notifications: Utilize push notifications for personalized offers and app updates.

- In-App Advertising: Place ads in relevant mobile apps to reach a broader audience.

4. Develop a Mobile Content Strategy

- Content Types: Focus on product videos, user reviews, and interactive content.

- Content Frequency: Plan a weekly schedule for content delivery.

- Content Calendar: Create a content calendar to organize campaigns around sales events and product launches.

5. Design Mobile-Friendly Content

- Responsive Design: Ensure all content is responsive and optimized for different screen sizes.

- Visual Appeal: Use high-quality images and clean layouts.

- Short and Engaging: Keep product descriptions concise and engaging.

6. Implement Mobile SEO

- Mobile-Friendly Website: Optimize the website for mobile devices, ensuring fast load times and easy navigation.

- Local SEO: Implement local SEO strategies to target users searching for products nearby.

- Voice Search Optimization: Optimize content for voice search queries.

7. Personalize the User Experience

- User Data: Use purchase history and browsing behavior to personalize the shopping experience.

- Dynamic Content: Deliver dynamic product recommendations based on user behavior.

- Segmentation: Segment users based on preferences and past purchases for targeted promotions.

8. Utilize Mobile Analytics

- Tracking and Measurement: Use mobile analytics to track app downloads, user engagement, and conversion rates.

- User Feedback: Gather feedback through app reviews and surveys.

- A/B Testing: Test different elements of push notifications and SMS messages.

9. Integrate with Other Marketing Channels

- Cross-Channel Integration: Integrate mobile marketing with email campaigns and social media promotions.

- Consistent Messaging: Ensure messaging is consistent across all channels.

- Unified Customer View: Track interactions across different channels for a seamless experience.

10. Monitor and Optimize

- Performance Metrics: Monitor metrics like app user retention and mobile-driven sales.

- Optimization: Regularly optimize campaigns based on performance data and user feedback.

- Stay Updated: Keep up with the latest trends and best practices in mobile marketing.

By following these best practices, your business can build a successful mobile marketing program that engages your audience, drives conversions, and supports your overall marketing goals. A well-implemented mobile marketing strategy provides a direct and effective way to reach your customers, personalize their experience, and promote your products or services through the devices they use most frequently.

Mobile Marketing Platforms for Managing Effective Campaigns

Managing an effective mobile marketing campaign requires choosing the right platforms that offer robust features, ease of use, and scalability. Here are some of the more popular systems available. I have gone through these below and highlighted their individual features and stated my opinion on why you should choose one platform over another.

HubSpot Mobile Marketing Hub

Features:

- **Comprehensive Marketing Automation:** HubSpot offers powerful automation tools that allow you to create, manage, and track multi-channel marketing campaigns, including mobile.

- **In-App Messaging:** Engage users directly within your app with targeted in-app messages.

- **SMS Marketing:** Send personalized SMS messages to your contacts and track their performance.

- **Push Notifications:** Deliver timely and relevant push notifications based on user behavior and preferences.

- **Analytics and Reporting:** Access detailed analytics to measure the effectiveness of your mobile marketing campaigns and make data-driven decisions.

Why Choose HubSpot:

- Integrated with HubSpot's CRM, making it easy to manage all aspects of your marketing and sales efforts in one place.

- User-friendly interface with extensive support and resources.

Braze

Features:

- **Real-Time Messaging:** Send real-time push notifications, in-app messages, and email campaigns based on user actions.

- **Personalization:** Use Braze's powerful personalization features to deliver highly relevant content to your users.

- **Customer Journeys:** Create and manage complex customer journeys with ease.

- **Analytics and Insights:** Gain deep insights into user behavior and campaign performance with comprehensive analytics tools.

- **A/B Testing:** Test different message variants to optimize your campaigns for better engagement.

Why Choose Braze:

- Known for its robust real-time messaging capabilities and ease of integration with other marketing tools.

- Ideal for businesses looking to deliver highly personalized and timely messages.

Airship (formerly Urban Airship)

Features:

- **Push Notifications:** Send targeted and personalized push notifications to engage users.

- **In-App Messaging:** Deliver contextual messages within your app to enhance user experience.

- **Mobile Wallet:** Create and manage mobile wallet passes for loyalty programs, coupons, and event tickets.

- **Automation:** Automate campaigns based on user behavior and lifecycle stages.

- **Analytics:** Access detailed performance analytics and insights to optimize your campaigns.

Why Choose Airship:

- Strong focus on push notifications and in-app messaging.

- Supports mobile wallet marketing, making it suitable for retail and event-based businesses.

Leanplum

Features:

- **Multi-Channel Messaging:** Manage push notifications, in-app messages, emails, and web push notifications from a single platform.

- **Personalization:** Use Leanplum's advanced personalization features to deliver relevant content to each user.

- **A/B Testing and Optimization:** Test and optimize different message variants to improve campaign performance.

- **Lifecycle Marketing:** Create automated campaigns tailored to different stages of the customer lifecycle.

- **Analytics:** Gain insights into user behavior and campaign effectiveness with powerful analytics tools.

Why Choose Leanplum:

- Known for its strong A/B testing and personalization capabilities.

- Ideal for businesses looking to create highly targeted and optimized mobile marketing campaigns.

OneSignal

Features:

- **Push Notifications:** Send push notifications to mobile and web users with ease.

- **In-App Messaging:** Engage users within your app with targeted in-app messages.

- **Email Marketing:** Manage email campaigns alongside push notifications and in-app messages.

- **Segmentation:** Segment your audience based on behavior, demographics, and other criteria.

- **Analytics and Reporting:** Access detailed reports and analytics to measure campaign performance.

Why Choose OneSignal:

- Offers a generous free tier, making it accessible for small businesses and startups.

- Easy to set up and use, with strong support for push notifications and in-app messaging.

MoEngage

Features:

- **Omni-Channel Campaigns:** Manage push notifications, in-app messages, emails, SMS, and web push notifications from a single platform.

- **Personalization:** Deliver personalized messages based on user behavior, preferences, and demographics.

- **Customer Journey Mapping:** Create and manage complex customer journeys with ease.

- **AI-Powered Insights:** Use AI-driven analytics to gain insights into user behavior and optimize your campaigns.

- **A/B Testing:** Test different message variants to identify the most effective strategies.

Why Choose MoEngage:

- Strong focus on AI-powered insights and personalization.

- Ideal for businesses looking to create cohesive omnichannel marketing campaigns.

Vibes

Features:

- **SMS and MMS Marketing:** Send targeted SMS and MMS messages to engage your audience.

- **Mobile Wallet:** Create and manage mobile wallet passes for loyalty programs and promotions.

- **Push Notifications:** Deliver timely push notifications to keep users engaged.

- **Rich Media Messaging:** Enhance your messages with rich media content such as images and videos.

- **Analytics:** Access detailed analytics to measure the effectiveness of your mobile marketing campaigns.

Why Choose Vibes:

- Specializes in SMS, MMS, and mobile wallet marketing.

- Ideal for retail and e-commerce businesses looking to engage customers through mobile messaging.

Choosing the right mobile marketing platform is crucial for managing effective mobile marketing campaigns. The platforms listed above offer a range of features to help you create, automate, and optimize your campaigns, ensuring you can engage your audience effectively and achieve your marketing goals. Whether you need robust automation, personalized messaging, or comprehensive analytics, these platforms provide the tools necessary to succeed in mobile marketing.

CHAPTER 10
Mobile Applications and Mobile Website

Mobile apps and mobile websites are both essential components of a business's digital presence, each serving distinct purposes and catering to different user needs:

Mobile Apps:

Mobile apps are software applications specifically designed to run on mobile devices such as smartphones and tablets. They are downloaded and installed from app stores (e.g., Apple App Store, Google Play Store) and reside locally on the user's device.

Key Characteristics:

1. Native Functionality: Mobile apps can leverage the device's hardware and software features, such as GPS, camera, and push notifications, to provide a seamless user experience.

2. Offline Access: Many mobile apps can function offline or with limited connectivity, allowing users to access certain features and content without an internet connection.

3. Personalization: Apps can store user preferences and behavior data locally, enabling personalized experiences tailored to individual users.

Benefits:

- Enhanced User Engagement: Mobile apps facilitate direct and personalized interactions with users through features like push notifications, in-app messages, and customized content delivery.

121

- Improved Performance: Apps typically offer faster loading times and smoother navigation compared to mobile websites, providing a more responsive and user-friendly experience.

- Brand Loyalty: By offering convenient access to services, exclusive content, and loyalty programs, apps can foster stronger relationships and repeat engagements with users.

Use Cases:

- E-commerce: Apps like Amazon and eBay provide seamless shopping experiences with features such as product browsing, reviews, and one-click purchasing.

- Social Media: Platforms like Facebook, Instagram, and TikTok offer rich media experiences, social interactions, and content creation tools through their mobile apps.

- Utilities: Apps such as banking apps (e.g., Chase Mobile), travel apps (e.g., Airbnb), and fitness apps (e.g., Strava) provide specialized functionalities tailored to specific user needs.

Best Practices for Creating and Managing A Mobile Application for Business

Creating and managing a mobile application (app) for business involves several best practices to ensure its success, user satisfaction, and alignment with business objectives. Here are some key practices to consider:

Planning and Strategy:

- Define Clear Objectives: Clearly outline the purpose and goals of the mobile app. Determine how the app will support business objectives, whether it's enhancing customer engagement, driving sales, improving operational efficiency, or offering unique services.

- Understand User Needs: Conduct thorough market research and user analysis to understand your target audience's preferences, behaviors, and pain points. Use this insight to tailor the app's features, design, and functionalities to meet user expectations.

- Choose the Right Platform: Decide whether to develop a native, web, or hybrid app based on your target audience, required features, budget, and time constraints. Native apps offer superior performance and user experience but require separate development for iOS and Android platforms.

Development and Design:

- Focus on User Experience (UX): Design an intuitive and user-friendly interface that prioritizes ease of navigation, accessibility, and responsiveness across different devices and screen sizes. Incorporate UX/UI best practices to ensure a seamless and enjoyable user experience.

- Performance Optimization: Optimize the app's performance to ensure fast loading times, smooth navigation, and minimal battery consumption. Conduct rigorous testing across various devices and network conditions to identify and address performance bottlenecks.

- Security and Data Privacy: Implement robust security measures to protect user data and ensure compliance with data protection regulations (e.g., GDPR, CCPA). Encrypt sensitive information, use secure authentication methods, and regularly update security protocols to mitigate risks.

Deployment and Marketing:

- Beta Testing and Feedback: Conduct beta testing with a diverse group of users to gather feedback and identify bugs or usability issues. Iterate based on user input to refine features and improve overall app functionality before the official launch.

- App Store Optimization (ASO): Optimize the app's listing on app stores (e.g., Apple App Store, Google Play Store) to improve discoverability and attract downloads. Use relevant keywords, compelling descriptions, high-quality visuals, and positive user reviews to enhance visibility.

- Promotion and User Acquisition: Develop a comprehensive marketing strategy to promote the app and acquire users. Leverage digital marketing channels, social media platforms, email campaigns, and partnerships to generate buzz, drive downloads, and encourage user engagement.

Maintenance and Support:

- Regular Updates and Enhancements: Continuously monitor app performance and user feedback to identify areas for improvement. Release regular updates with new features, bug fixes, and performance optimizations to keep the app relevant and maintain user satisfaction.

- Customer Support and Engagement: Provide responsive customer support channels within the app to address user inquiries, feedback, and technical issues promptly. Implement in-app messaging, FAQs, and community forums to foster user engagement and loyalty.

- Analytics and Performance Monitoring: Integrate analytics tools (e.g., Google Analytics, Firebase Analytics) to track user behavior, app usage metrics, and performance indicators. Use data-driven insights to measure app success, optimize features, and make informed decisions for future updates.

By adhering to these best practices throughout the lifecycle of your mobile application, businesses can create a compelling, user-centric app that drives engagement, enhances brand reputation, and contributes to overall business growth.

Mobile Websites:

Definition: A mobile website is a version of a website optimized for viewing and navigation on mobile devices. It is accessed through a web browser and adapts its layout and content to fit various screen sizes.

Key Characteristics:

- Responsive Design: Mobile websites use responsive web design techniques to adjust content dynamically based on the device's screen size, orientation, and capabilities.

- Browser-Based Access: Users access mobile websites through web browsers (e.g., Chrome, Safari) without the need for downloading or installing additional software.

- Search Engine Accessibility: Mobile websites are indexed by search engines and can drive organic traffic through search engine optimization (SEO) strategies.

Benefits:

- Accessibility: Mobile websites are universally accessible across different devices and platforms, ensuring broad reach and convenience for users.

- Cost-Effectiveness: Developing and maintaining a mobile website can be more cost-effective than building and updating a mobile app, especially for businesses with limited resources.

- SEO and Discoverability: Mobile websites contribute to SEO efforts and improve search engine rankings, driving organic traffic and increasing visibility among potential customers.

Use Cases:

- Informational Sites: Websites for news publications (e.g., BBC News), educational institutions, and corporate entities provide content, updates, and resources optimized for mobile viewing.

- Transactional Sites: Retailers and service providers (e.g., Walmart and Airbnb) use mobile websites for online shopping, reservations, and account management.

- Content Platforms: Blogging sites (e.g., Medium), video streaming services (e.g., YouTube), and social networks (e.g., Twitter) offer mobile-friendly interfaces for content consumption and interaction.

Choosing Between Mobile Apps and Mobile Websites:

- Purpose and Functionality: Consider whether your business requires the advanced features, offline capabilities, and personalized experiences that mobile apps can offer or if a responsive and accessible mobile website meets your goals.

- User Preferences: Understand your target audience's preferences and behaviors regarding mobile usage to determine which platform will provide the best user experience and engagement.

- Budget and Resources: Evaluate the costs, time, and resources required for the development, maintenance, and promotion of both mobile apps and websites, aligning with your business's financial capabilities and strategic priorities.

While both mobile apps and mobile websites play integral roles in a business's digital strategy, understanding their distinct characteristics, benefits, and use cases is essential for making informed decisions that align with business objectives and user expectations.

CHAPTER 11
How To Create a Brand Marketing

Brand marketing is a strategic approach that focuses on creating and promoting a brand's image, an identity for your business, and establishing a reputation to build strong, long-lasting relationships with current and future customers Unlike product marketing, which emphasizes individual products, brand marketing aims to establish an emotional connection between the brand and its audience, fostering loyalty and trust. It involves various activities, such as defining brand values, creating a unique brand voice, and consistently communicating the brand message across multiple channels.

Key Components of Brand Marketing

Brand Identity:

The visual elements of a brand, such as a logo, color scheme, typography, and packaging, make it recognizable.

1. **Brand Positioning:**
   o The strategic process of defining the brand's unique place in the market and how it differs from competitors.

2. **Brand Messaging:**
   o The language, tone, and voice are used to convey the brand's values, mission, and promise to its audience.

3. **Brand Experience:**
   o The overall perception and interaction consumers have with the brand, including customer service, online presence, and product quality.

4. Brand Loyalty:

o The degree of attachment and preference consumers have toward a brand often results in repeat purchases and advocacy.

Why Should a Business Consider a Brand Strategy

A brand strategy is a long-term plan designed to help a business achieve specific goals related to brand development, identity, and recognition. Here are several reasons why a business should consider implementing a brand strategy:

Stand Out in the Market: A well-defined brand strategy helps a business stand out in a crowded market. By clearly articulating what makes your brand unique and valuable, you can differentiate yourself from competitors.

Create a Unique Value Proposition: A brand strategy enables you to create a unique value proposition that highlights your strengths and the benefits you offer that others do not.

Emotional Connection: Strong branding creates an emotional connection with customers, fostering loyalty and long-term relationships. When customers identify with your brand's values and mission, they are more likely to remain loyal.

Consistency Builds Trust: Consistent branding across all touchpoints builds trust with your audience. When customers see the same message and quality consistently, it reinforces their trust in your brand.

Memorable Identity: A cohesive brand strategy helps create a memorable brand identity that customers can easily recognize. This includes your logo, color scheme, typography, and overall design language.

Increased Visibility: Consistent and strategic branding increases your visibility in the market. Over time, your brand becomes more recognizable, making it easier for customers to remember and choose your products or services.

Aligned Marketing Campaigns: A clear brand strategy ensures that all marketing efforts are aligned with your brand's goals and values. This alignment makes marketing campaigns more effective and cohesive.

Efficient Use of Resources: With a brand strategy in place, marketing teams can work more efficiently, focusing their efforts on campaigns that support the brand's objectives and resonate with the target audience.

Employer Branding: A strong brand strategy not only attracts customers but also helps attract top talent. Prospective employees are more likely to be drawn to a company with a strong, positive brand identity.

Employee Engagement: When employees understand and believe in the brand's mission and values, they are more engaged and motivated. This leads to higher productivity and lower turnover rates.

Perceived Value: Strong branding can enhance the perceived value of your products or services, allowing you to command higher prices. Customers are often willing to pay a premium for brands they trust and perceive as high-quality.

Brand Equity: Over time, a strong brand strategy builds brand equity, which is the value derived from consumer perception of the brand. This equity can translate into financial benefits, including the ability to charge higher prices.

Easier Market Entry: A well-established brand makes it easier to enter new markets and launch new products. Customers who are already familiar with and trust your brand are more likely to try your new offers.

Brand Extensions: A strong brand can support brand extensions, where you leverage your existing brand to introduce new products or services. This strategy can help reduce the risks associated with launching new ventures.

Vision and Direction: A brand strategy provides a clear vision and direction for the business. It helps guide decision-making and ensures that all business activities are aligned with the brand's long-term goals.

Resilience in Adversity: Strong brands are more resilient during economic downturns and crises. Customers' loyalty to trusted brands can help sustain business through challenging times.

A well-executed brand strategy is essential for any business looking to establish a strong market presence, build customer loyalty, and achieve long-term success. It differentiates your brand, builds trust, enhances recognition, and supports all marketing efforts. By aligning your business activities with a clear and cohesive brand strategy, you can create a powerful brand that resonates with customers and stands the test of time.

Below are a few examples of consumer products and how they were able to implement brand marketing into their business.

Nike: Just Do It

Strategy:

- **Brand Identity:** Nike's iconic swoosh logo and bold typography are instantly recognizable.

- **Brand Positioning:** Nike positions itself as a premium athletic brand that inspires and empowers athletes of all levels.

- **Brand Messaging:** The slogan "Just Do It" encourages people to push their limits and pursue their goals, aligning with Nike's mission to bring inspiration and innovation to every athlete.

- **Brand Experience:** Nike provides a seamless shopping experience through its website, mobile app, and physical stores. It also offers personalized recommendations and training programs.

- **Brand Loyalty:** Through high-profile endorsements, sponsorships, and community engagement, Nike has built a loyal customer base that advocates for the brand.

Result: Nike has become synonymous with athletic performance and innovation, maintaining a strong market presence and customer loyalty.

Apple: Think Different

Strategy:

- Brand Identity: Apple's minimalist design, sleek product aesthetics, and the iconic Apple logo are easily identifiable.

- Brand Positioning: Apple positions itself as a premium technology brand that offers innovative and user-friendly products.

- Brand Messaging: The "Think Different" campaign emphasizes creativity, innovation, and challenging the status quo.

- Brand Experience: Apple provides a unique and cohesive customer experience across its products, retail stores, and online platforms.

- Brand Loyalty: Apple's ecosystem of products and services, combined with exceptional customer support and frequent software updates, fosters deep brand loyalty.

Result: Apple has a devoted customer base and is seen as a leader in technological innovation, often setting trends in the industry.

Coca-Cola: Share a Coke

Strategy:

- Brand Identity: Coca-Cola's classic red and white color scheme and distinct logo are globally recognized.

- Brand Positioning: Coca-Cola positions itself as a brand that brings happiness and refreshment to consumers.

- Brand Messaging: The "Share a Coke" campaign personalized bottles with popular names, encouraging people to share a Coke with friends and loved ones.

- Brand Experience: Coca-Cola creates memorable experiences through its advertising, packaging, and participation in events and social causes.

- Brand Loyalty: The brand's consistent quality, wide availability, and nostalgic marketing efforts maintain strong customer loyalty.

Result: Coca-Cola remains one of the most recognized and loved brands worldwide, with a significant market share in the beverage industry.

Dove: Real Beauty

Strategy:

- Brand Identity: Dove's clean, simple design and the iconic dove symbol convey purity and care.

- Brand Positioning: Dove positions itself as a brand that promotes real beauty and self-esteem among women.

- Brand Messaging: The "Real Beauty" campaign challenges traditional beauty standards and celebrates diversity and body positivity.

- Brand Experience: Dove engages with its audience through authentic storytelling, social media campaigns, and partnerships with organizations that promote self-esteem.

- Brand Loyalty: By aligning its values with those of its audience, Dove builds strong emotional connections and loyalty.

Result: Dove has successfully differentiated itself in the crowded beauty market and is seen as a champion of real beauty and self-confidence.

Tesla: Accelerating the World's Transition to Sustainable Energy

Strategy:

- Brand Identity: Tesla's sleek logo and futuristic design aesthetic reflect its innovation and forward-thinking vision.

- Brand Positioning: Tesla positions itself as a leader in sustainable energy and electric vehicles, offering cutting-edge technology and performance.

- Brand Messaging: The mission statement "Accelerating the World's Transition to Sustainable Energy" communicates Tesla's commitment to environmental sustainability.

- Brand Experience: Tesla offers a unique buying experience through its direct-to-consumer sales model, online ordering, and educational content about sustainable energy.

- Brand Loyalty: Tesla's emphasis on innovation, high-quality products, and a strong brand community fosters deep loyalty and advocacy among its customers.

Result: Tesla has established itself as a disruptive force in the automotive industry, with a strong brand identity and a loyal customer base passionate about sustainability.

Brand marketing is crucial for building a strong, recognizable brand that resonates with consumers on an emotional level. By defining a clear brand identity, positioning, messaging, and experience, businesses can cultivate brand loyalty and stand out in a competitive market. The examples of Nike, Apple, Coca-Cola, Dove, and Tesla illustrate how effective brand marketing can drive customer engagement, loyalty, and long-term success.

Best Practice: Building a Brand Strategy for Your Business

A strong brand strategy is essential for defining and communicating your business's unique identity, values, and offerings to your target audience. It involves aligning your brand's purpose with your business objectives to create a cohesive and memorable brand experience. Here's a step-by-step outline of best practices for building a brand strategy:

1. Define Your Brand Identity

- Brand Purpose: Clarify the fundamental reason for your business's existence beyond making a profit. Define what drives your company and why it matters to your customers.

- Brand Vision: Envision where you want your brand to be in the future and how you aspire to impact your industry or community.

- Brand Values: Identify the core values that guide your business decisions and define the principles you stand for.

2. Conduct Market Research

- Target Audience: Define your ideal customer persona(s) by demographics, behaviors, needs, and preferences. Understand their pain points and motivations.

- Competitive Analysis: Analyze your competitors' branding strategies, market positioning, strengths, and weaknesses to identify opportunities for differentiation.

3. Develop Your Brand Positioning

- Unique Selling Proposition (USP): Determine what sets your brand apart from competitors. Identify the specific benefits and value propositions that resonate most with your target audience.

- Brand Promise: Craft a compelling promise that communicates what customers can expect from your brand consistently.

4. Create Brand Messaging

- Brand Voice: Define the tone, style, and personality of your brand's communication. Ensure it aligns with your brand values and resonates with your target audience.

- Tagline and Slogans: Develop memorable and impactful taglines or slogans that encapsulate your brand's essence and USP.

5. Design Your Visual Identity

- Logo Design: Create a distinctive and visually appealing logo that reflects your brand's personality and values. Ensure it is versatile and works across different platforms and mediums.

- Color Palette: Choose a cohesive color scheme that evokes the desired emotions and associations related to your brand.

- Typography: Select fonts that complement your brand's voice and enhance readability.

6. Build Brand Awareness

- Content Marketing: Develop valuable and relevant content that educates, entertains, or inspires your audience while subtly reinforcing your brand's values and offerings.

- Social Media Presence: Leverage social media platforms to engage with your audience, share your brand story, and build relationships.

- Public Relations: Generate positive media coverage and manage your brand's reputation through strategic PR initiatives.

7. Implement Brand Consistency

- Brand Guidelines: Create comprehensive brand guidelines that outline rules for logo usage, color schemes, typography, and tone of voice. Ensure consistency across all communication channels and touchpoints.

- Employee Training: Educate and empower employees to embody your brand values and deliver a consistent brand experience in their interactions with customers.

8. Monitor and Adapt

- Brand Performance Metrics: Track key performance indicators (KPIs) such as brand awareness, brand sentiment, customer loyalty, and market share.

- Feedback and Insights: Gather feedback from customers, employees, and stakeholders to understand perceptions of your brand and identify areas for improvement.

- Adaptation: Continuously refine your brand strategy based on data-driven insights, market trends, and evolving customer preferences.

Example of a Business Brand Strategy: Fashion Brand

1. Define Your Brand Identity

- Brand Purpose: Empower eco-conscious consumers to make sustainable fashion choices.

- Brand Vision: Lead the fashion industry towards sustainable practices and ethical production standards.

- Brand Values: Sustainability, transparency, and innovation.

2. Conduct Market Research

- Target Audience: Millennials and Gen Z consumers who prioritize sustainability and ethical practices in their purchasing decisions.

- Competitive Analysis: Analyze competitors offering sustainable fashion, highlighting gaps and differentiation opportunities.

3. Develop Your Brand Positioning

- Unique Selling Proposition (USP): Offering stylish, eco-friendly fashion that does not compromise on quality or ethics.

- Brand Promise: Commitment to transparency in sourcing, manufacturing processes, and materials used.

4. Create Brand Messaging

- Brand Voice: Authentic, empowering, and educational about sustainable fashion choices.

- Tagline and Slogans: "Fashion for a Sustainable Future" or "Style with Purpose."

5. Design Your Visual Identity

- Logo Design: Incorporate elements symbolizing sustainability (e.g., leaf, recycled materials) in a modern and minimalist style.

- Color Palette: Earth tones and shades of green and blue to convey eco-friendliness and natural elements.

- Typography: Clean and readable fonts that reflect a contemporary yet timeless aesthetic.

6. Build Brand Awareness

- Content Marketing: Blog posts on sustainable fashion tips, eco-friendly lifestyle guides, and behind-the-scenes stories.

- Social Media Presence: Showcase sustainable practices, customer stories, and fashion trends on Instagram, TikTok, and Pinterest.

- Public Relations: Collaborate with environmental NGOs, participate in eco-fashion events, and secure media coverage on sustainable initiatives.

7. Implement Brand Consistency

- Brand Guidelines: Document guidelines for logo usage, color codes, brand voice, and content style across platforms.

- Employee Training: Train staff on sustainable practices, brand values, and customer engagement strategies.

8. Monitor and Adapt

- Brand Performance Metrics: Track social media engagement rates, website traffic, customer feedback on sustainability efforts, and sales of eco-friendly collections.

- Feedback and Insights: Conduct surveys and gather customer feedback on perceptions of brand sustainability and product satisfaction.

- Adaptation: Adjust marketing strategies based on insights, such as expanding product lines or enhancing sustainability communications.

A well-defined brand strategy helps your business differentiate itself in a competitive market, build customer loyalty, and create meaningful connections with your target audience. By following these best practices and continuously refining your approach, you can establish a strong brand presence that resonates with customers and drives long-term success.

Implementing a branding strategy is essential for creating a strong, recognizable brand that resonates with your target audience. By defining your brand identity, developing a cohesive strategy, and maintaining consistent branding across all touchpoints, you can build brand loyalty, enhance recognition, and achieve long-term business success. Continuous monitoring and optimization ensure that your brand remains relevant and effective in a dynamic market.

CHAPTER 12
Understanding Digital Marketing Influencers

Digital marketing influencers, also known as social media influencers, are individuals who have established credibility and a substantial following on social media platforms. They use their influence to shape the opinions and behaviors of their audience through content creation and engagement. In today's marketing strategy, digital influencers play a crucial role in helping brands connect with their target audience in a more authentic and relatable way.

Characteristics of Digital Influencers

- **Credibility:** Influencers are seen as trustworthy sources of information within their niche or industry. They build credibility through consistent, honest, and high-quality content.

- **Reach:** Influencers can reach a large and often engaged audience. Their followers trust their recommendations and are likely to act on them.

- **Engagement:** Influencers have high levels of engagement with their followers, including likes, comments, shares, and direct messages. This engagement is crucial for building strong connections with the audience.

- **Niche Focus:** Many influencers specialize in specific niches, such as fashion, beauty, fitness, technology, travel, or food. This specialization helps them attract and retain followers interested in those topics.

- **Content Creation:** Influencers are skilled content creators, producing videos, photos, blog posts, and other media that resonate with their audience. They often use a personal and relatable approach to content.

Types of Digital Influencers

- **Mega-Influencers:** Typically have over a million followers. They are often celebrities or well-known public figures.

- Example: Kylie Jenner, who has millions of followers and significant influence in beauty and fashion.

- **Macro-Influencers:** Have between 100,000 and a million followers. They are often professionals or experts in their field.

- Example: Marcus Butler, a YouTuber with a large following in the lifestyle and fitness niche.

- **Micro-Influencers:** Have between 10,000 and 100,000 followers. They are usually seen as more relatable and approachable than mega-influencers.

- Example: A local fitness coach with a dedicated following on Instagram.

- **Nano-Influencers:** Have fewer than 10,000 followers. Despite their smaller audience, they often have high engagement rates and strong personal connections with their followers.

- **Example:** A passionate home cook sharing recipes and cooking tips on social media.

Benefits of Using Digital Influencers in Marketing Strategy

Businesses should consider implementing a digital influencer strategy as part of their marketing efforts, especially if their target audience is active on social media platforms. Here are several reasons why leveraging digital influencers can be beneficial for businesses:

o **Enhanced Credibility and Trust:** Collaborating with influencers who are trusted by their audience can lend credibility to your brand and build trust with potential customers.

o **Increased Reach and Visibility:** Influencers can help you reach a wider audience, including demographics that might be difficult to target through traditional advertising.

o **Authentic Content Creation:** Influencers create authentic and relatable content that resonates with their audience, making your brand's message more impactful.

o **Higher Engagement Rates:** Influencers typically have higher engagement rates compared to brand-owned channels. Their followers are more likely to interact with and share influencer-generated content.

o **Targeted Marketing:** Working with influencers who specialize in specific niches allows for highly targeted marketing, reaching people who are genuinely interested in your products or services.

Examples of Digital Influencer Marketing Campaigns

- **Fashion Industry:**

- o **Campaign:** H&M partnered with fashion influencers to promote their new clothing line.

- o **Strategy:** Influencers shared photos and videos wearing H&M outfits, along with personal styling tips.

- o **Results:** The campaign increased brand visibility, drove traffic to H&M's online store, and boosted sales of the promoted clothing line.

- **Beauty Industry:**

  - o **Campaign:** L'Oréal collaborated with beauty influencers to launch a new line of makeup products.

  - o **Strategy:** Influencers created makeup tutorials and reviews, showcasing the products and demonstrating their use.

  - o **Results:** The campaign generated buzz, leading to high engagement and significant increases in product sales.

- **Travel Industry:**

  - o **Campaign:** Tourism boards partnered with travel influencers to promote destinations.

  - o **Strategy:** Influencers documented their travel experiences through blog posts, social media updates, and vlogs, highlighting the attractions and activities.

  - o **Results:** The campaign enhanced the destination's visibility, attracting more tourists and boosting local tourism businesses.

- **Fitness Industry:**

- o **Campaign:** A fitness apparel brand collaborated with fitness influencers to promote their workout gear.

- o **Strategy:** Influencers posted workout routines, wearing the brand's apparel, and offered discount codes to their followers.

- o **Results:** The campaign drove brand awareness, increased social media engagement, and resulted in higher sales.

- **Technology Industry:**

  - o **Campaign:** A tech company partnered with tech influencers to review and demonstrate their latest gadgets.

  - o **Strategy:** Influencers created detailed unboxing videos, reviews, and tutorials, explaining the features and benefits of the products.

  - o **Results:** The campaign generated excitement and anticipation, leading to higher pre-order numbers and sales upon release.

Steps to Identify a Digital Influencer

Identifying the right digital influencer for your business involves a strategic approach to ensure alignment with your brand values, target audience, and marketing goals. Here are steps to help businesses identify suitable digital influencers:

- **Define Your Target Audience:**

  - o Start by clearly defining who your target audience is. Consider demographics (age, gender, location), interests, behaviors, and preferences relevant to your product or service.

- **Set Clear Objectives:**

  o Determine what you want to achieve through influencer marketing. Whether it's increasing brand awareness, driving sales, enhancing credibility, or engaging a specific audience segment, having clear objectives will guide your influencer search.

- **Research Relevant Platforms:**

  o Identify social media platforms where your target audience is most active. Popular platforms include Instagram, YouTube, TikTok, Facebook, Twitter, and LinkedIn. Different platforms may be more effective depending on your business and audience demographics.

- **Use Influencer Tools and Platforms:**

  o Utilize influencer marketing platforms and tools to discover influencers who align with your criteria. These tools provide insights into influencers' audience demographics, engagement rates, content style, and previous collaborations.

- **Evaluate Influencer Authenticity and Engagement:**

  o Look for influencers who demonstrate authenticity and have genuine engagement with their audience. Engagement metrics such as likes, comments, shares, and views can indicate how active and responsive their followers are.

- **Check Content Quality and Alignment:**

  o Review the influencer's content to ensure it aligns with your brand's values, aesthetics, and messaging.

Assess the quality of their photos, videos, captions, and overall storytelling ability.

- **Consider Influencer Reputation and Background:**
  - o Research the influencer's reputation, credibility, and any past controversies that may impact your brand's image. Check their follower growth rate, audience demographics, and overall online presence.

- **Assess Influencer Reach and Impact:**
  - o Evaluate the influencer's reach in terms of follower count and geographical distribution. Determine how influential they are within their niche or industry and their ability to drive actions among their followers.

- **Review Past Campaigns and Partnerships:**
  - o Examine the influencer's previous collaborations and campaigns with other brands. Evaluate the success of these partnerships in achieving similar objectives to yours and whether they align with your brand's values.

- **Engage in Personalized Outreach:**
  - o Reach out to shortlisted influencers with personalized messages that highlight why you believe they are a good fit for your brand. Clearly outline your campaign goals, expectations, and any collaboration terms.

By following these steps, businesses can effectively identify digital influencers who can help amplify their brand message, reach their target audience authentically, and achieve their marketing objectives through influencer collaborations.

Challenges of Digital Influencer Marketing

Finding a suitable digital influencer for your business can be both challenging and time-consuming, depending on various factors such as your niche, target audience, and campaign objectives. Here are some key challenges businesses typically face when searching for digital influencers:

1. **Finding the Right Influencer:**

   o It can be challenging to identify influencers who align with your brand values and have a genuine following.

2. **Authenticity Concerns:**

   o Overly promotional content can come across as inauthentic, leading to a loss of trust among followers.

3. **Measuring ROI:**

   o Tracking the return on investment (ROI) of influencer campaigns can be difficult, especially if the goals are related to brand awareness rather than direct sales.

4. **Regulatory Compliance:**

   o Ensuring compliance with advertising regulations, such as disclosure requirements for sponsored content, is essential to avoid legal issues.

5. **Managing Relationships:**

   o Building and maintaining strong relationships with influencers requires ongoing effort and clear communication.

Digital influencers are a powerful tool in today's marketing strategy, offering brands the opportunity to connect with their target audience in an authentic and impactful way. By leveraging the reach, credibility, and engagement of influencers, businesses can enhance brand awareness, build trust, and drive sales. However, successful influencer marketing requires careful planning, execution, and measurement to navigate the challenges and maximize the benefits.

Best Practice: Leveraging Digital Influencers for Your Business

Incorporating digital influencers into your marketing strategy can significantly enhance brand awareness, credibility, and engagement with your target audience. Here's a step-by-step outline of best practices for effectively leveraging digital influencers for your business:

1. Set Clear Objectives and Goals

- **Define Goals:** Determine what you aim to achieve by collaborating with influencers, such as increasing brand visibility, driving website traffic, boosting sales, or improving brand perception.

- **Quantifiable Metrics:** Establish measurable key performance indicators (KPIs) to track the success of influencer campaigns, such as engagement rates, click-through rates, conversions, and ROI.

2. Identify Your Target Audience

- **Audience Persona:** Define your ideal customer demographics, interests, behaviors, and preferences to identify influencers whose followers align with your target audience.

- **Relevance:** Choose influencers whose content and values resonate with your brand's identity and mission to ensure authenticity and credibility.

3. Research and Select Relevant Influencers

- **Influencer Categories:** Consider different types of influencers based on their reach and impact, such as macro-influencers (celebrities with large followings), micro-influencers (niche experts with engaged audiences), and nano-influencers (local influencers with a smaller but highly targeted audience).

- **Performance Analysis:** Evaluate influencers based on their past collaborations, audience engagement rates, content quality, authenticity, and alignment with your brand values.

- **Platform Suitability:** Choose influencers who are active on platforms where your target audience spends their time, such as Instagram, YouTube, TikTok, or blogs.

4. Build Authentic Relationships

- **Personalized Outreach:** Approach influencers with personalized messages that demonstrate your understanding of their content and audience.

- **Mutual Benefits:** Clearly communicate the benefits of collaboration, such as exclusive access, product samples, or financial compensation, while respecting their creative freedom.

- **Long-term Partnerships:** Foster ongoing relationships with influencers who align with your brand values for consistent and authentic advocacy.

5. **Co-create Compelling Content**

- **Creative Collaboration:** Collaborate with influencers to develop engaging and authentic content that resonates with their audience while highlighting your brand's unique selling points.

- **Storytelling:** Encourage influencers to integrate your brand naturally into their narrative or lifestyle, showcasing product features, benefits, or brand values organically.

- **Visual Appeal:** Leverage influencers' creative skills to produce high-quality images, videos, reviews, tutorials, or sponsored posts that captivate their followers.

6. **Monitor and Measure Performance**

- **Performance Tracking:** Utilize tracking tools and analytics to monitor the performance of influencer campaigns in real-time, including reach, impressions, engagement metrics, and conversions.

- **ROI Calculation:** Calculate the return on investment (ROI) by comparing campaign costs with generated revenue, customer acquisition, or brand lift metrics.

- **Feedback and Optimization:** Gather feedback from influencers and audience responses to optimize future campaigns, identify successful strategies, and address any challenges or concerns.

7. Comply with Regulations and Guidelines

- **Disclosure and Transparency:** Ensure influencers disclose sponsored content and partnerships clearly and transparently to comply with advertising regulations and build trust with their audience.

- **Legal Compliance:** Familiarize yourself with local and international regulations governing influencer marketing, including FTC guidelines in the United States, to avoid legal repercussions.

8. Nurture Community Engagement

- **Engage with Audience:** Monitor comments, mentions, and interactions on influencer posts to engage with their audience authentically, answer questions, and address feedback.

- **User-generated Content (UGC):** Encourage influencers' followers to share their experiences with your brand through contests, hashtags, or challenges, fostering a sense of community and advocacy.

Example Business: Fitness Apparel Brand

1. Set Clear Objectives and Goals

- **Goals:** Increase brand awareness among fitness enthusiasts and drive online sales of new product lines.

- **KPIs:** Measure engagement rates, click-through rates from influencer posts, and sales attributed to influencer campaigns.

2. Identify Your Target Audience

- **Audience Persona:** Young adults aged 18-35 interested in fitness, health, and active lifestyles.

- **Influencer Fit:** Partner with fitness trainers, athletes, and lifestyle bloggers with a strong presence on Instagram and YouTube.

3. Research and Select Relevant Influencers

- **Selection Criteria:** Choose micro-influencers with 10,000-50,000 followers who specialize in fitness and wellness content.

- **Performance Analysis:** Evaluate influencers based on engagement rates, authenticity of content, and alignment with the brand's values of health, fitness, and sustainability.

4. Build Authentic Relationships

- **Outreach Strategy:** Reach out to influencers with personalized pitches highlighting mutual benefits, such as product sponsorships and affiliate partnerships.

- **Relationship Building:** Cultivate long-term partnerships by offering ongoing collaborations and exclusive access to new product launches.

5. Co-create Compelling Content

- **Content Collaboration:** Collaborate with influencers to create engaging content, including workout routines featuring your apparel, fitness tips, and lifestyle posts.

- **Visual Appeal:** Leverage high-quality images and videos showcasing the brand's apparel in action during workouts or daily activities.

6. Monitor and Measure Performance

- **Performance Metrics:** Track influencer campaign performance through analytics tools, measuring reach, impressions, engagement, and referral traffic to the brand's website.

- **ROI Analysis:** Calculate ROI by comparing sales attributed to influencer campaigns against campaign costs and customer acquisition metrics.

7. Comply with Regulations and Guidelines

- **Transparency:** Ensure influencers disclose partnerships with clear hashtags (#ad, #sponsored) and comply with FTC guidelines for transparency in advertising.

8. Nurture Community Engagement

- **Community Interaction:** Engage with followers in the comments section of influencer posts, responding to questions and encouraging user-generated content with branded hashtags.

By following these best practices, your business can effectively leverage digital influencers to amplify brand reach, engage with target audiences authentically, and drive measurable results. Strategic partnerships with influencers who align with your brand values and resonate with your audience can enhance brand credibility, foster community engagement, and ultimately contribute to business growth and success in the digital age.

A PRACTICAL GUIDE TO DIGITAL MARKETING

Top of Form

Bottom of Form

CHAPTER 13
What Is Channel Marketing

Channel marketing, also known as distribution marketing, involves using various intermediaries, third-party partnerships, or resellers to reach customers and distribute and sell products or services effectively. It plays a crucial role in growing a business by expanding market reach, optimizing distribution efficiency, and leveraging the strengths of the existing channel partners. Here's a detailed description of channel marketing and its strategic application in business growth:

Channel marketing focuses on the distribution and promotion of products or services through intermediaries or channels rather than selling directly to end-users. These channels can include distributors, retailers, wholesalers, agents, resellers, and online marketplaces. The primary goal is to ensure products reach target customers efficiently while leveraging the expertise and reach of channel partners.

How Channel Marketing Can Grow a Business:

1. **Expanded Market Reach:**

   o Access to Diverse Markets: Leveraging established channels allows businesses to access new geographic regions, niche markets, or customer segments that may be challenging to reach directly.

   o Market Penetration: By partnering with distributors or retailers with extensive networks, businesses can penetrate markets quickly and increase brand visibility.

2. **Optimized Distribution Efficiency:**

o Logistics and Fulfillment: Channel partners manage logistics, warehousing, and order fulfillment, reducing operational complexities and costs for businesses.

o Scalability: Scaling distribution becomes more manageable as businesses tap into existing channel infrastructures and capabilities.

3. **Market Expertise and Local Knowledge:**

o Customer Insights: Channel partners often possess valuable insights into local market preferences, consumer behaviors, and competitive landscapes, informing product customization and marketing strategies.

o Brand Representation: Partners act as brand ambassadors, providing personalized customer service and enhancing brand credibility through their expertise and relationships.

4. **Strategic Alliances and Collaborations:**

o Co-marketing Opportunities: Collaborating with channel partners on joint marketing campaigns, promotions, or events amplifies brand awareness and drives customer engagement.

o Cross-selling and Up-selling: Partnerships enable cross-selling complementary products or services, increasing average order value and customer lifetime value.

5. **Cost Efficiency and Risk Mitigation:**

o Reduced Marketing Costs: Sharing marketing expenses with channel partners minimizes the financial burden of customer acquisition and promotional activities.

o Risk Sharing: Distributing risk across multiple channels diversifies revenue streams and mitigates the impact of market fluctuations or disruptions.

Managing a channel marketing program effectively involves strategic planning, clear communication, and proactive management of relationships with channel partners. Here are essential steps and best practices to best manage a channel marketing program:

Steps to Best Manage a Channel Marketing Program:

Develop a Clear Channel Strategy:

o Define objectives, target markets, and key performance indicators (KPIs) for the channel marketing program.

o Align channel strategies with overall business goals and sales objectives.

Select and Onboard Channel Partners:

o Identify potential channel partners based on their market reach, customer base, capabilities, and alignment with your brand values.

o Establish selection criteria and onboard partners through formal agreements, training programs, and joint planning sessions.

Provide Comprehensive Partner Enablement:

o Offer training sessions, product demonstrations, and resources to educate partners about your products or services.

- o Equip partners with marketing collateral, sales tools, and support materials to facilitate effective promotion and sales.

Joint Planning and Goal Setting:

- o Collaborate with channel partners to develop joint business plans and set mutual goals and objectives.

- o Define roles, responsibilities, and expectations for both parties to ensure alignment and accountability.

Implement Coordinated Marketing Strategies:

- o Develop co-marketing campaigns, promotions, and incentive programs to drive demand generation and lead generation activities.

- o Leverage partners' local expertise and customer insights to tailor marketing messages and strategies for specific markets.

Monitor Performance and Provide Support:

- o Establish metrics and KPIs to measure channel performance, including sales metrics, market penetration, and customer satisfaction.

- o Use analytics and reporting tools to track progress, identify trends, and assess the effectiveness of marketing initiatives.

Regular Communication and Relationship Management:

- o Maintain open communication channels with channel partners through regular meetings, updates, and feedback sessions.

o Address concerns, provide timely support, and collaborate on resolving issues to maintain strong relationships.

Evaluate and Optimize Channel Programs:

o Conduct periodic reviews and performance evaluations to assess program effectiveness and ROI.

o Gather feedback from partners and stakeholders to identify areas for improvement and refine channel strategies accordingly.

Resources Needed To Create and Manage a Channel Marketing Program

o Creating and managing a channel marketing program requires a combination of strategic resources, tools, and capabilities to reach target customers through distribution partners effectively. Here are the key resources needed to establish and manage a successful channel marketing program:

1. Human Resources:

• Channel Manager: Responsible for overseeing the program, managing partner relationships, and coordinating marketing efforts.

• Marketing Team: Supports the development of marketing strategies, creates promotional materials, and executes campaigns in collaboration with channel partners.

• Sales Team: Works closely with partners to drive sales, provide product training, and facilitate customer support.

2. Financial Resources:

- Budget Allocation: Funds allocated for partner incentives, co-marketing campaigns, promotional activities, and operational expenses.

- Co-op Funds: Financial assistance provided to partners for joint marketing initiatives, advertising, and promotional efforts.

3. Technology and Tools:

- CRM (Customer Relationship Management) System: Manages partner relationships, tracks interactions, and monitors performance metrics.

- Marketing Automation Tools: Automates email campaigns, lead nurturing, and marketing workflows to streamline processes and improve efficiency.

- Analytics and Reporting Tools: Provides insights into campaign performance, sales data, ROI metrics, and partner contribution.

4. Training and Support:

- Partner Onboarding Programs: Provide training sessions, product demonstrations, and sales enablement resources to educate partners about products/services.

- Technical Support: Offers assistance with product integration, troubleshooting, and customer inquiries to ensure partners deliver a positive customer experience.

5. Marketing Collateral and Resources:

- Branding Guidelines: Defines brand identity, messaging, and visual elements to maintain consistency across all marketing materials.

- Co-marketing Materials: Includes brochures, presentations, case studies, videos, and digital assets co-created with partners for promotional purposes.

- Sales Tools: Provides product datasheets, pricing guides, FAQs, and competitive analysis to support partners in sales conversations.

6. Legal and Compliance Support:

- Contracts and Agreements: Formalizes partnerships with legally binding agreements outlining terms, responsibilities, and expectations.

- Regulatory Compliance: Ensures adherence to industry regulations, data protection laws, and intellectual property rights when conducting marketing activities.

7. Performance Metrics and Evaluation:

- KPIs (Key Performance Indicators): Defines metrics such as sales revenue, market share, lead conversion rates, and customer acquisition costs to measure program effectiveness.

- Performance Monitoring: Regularly monitors partner performance, tracks progress against goals, and identifies areas for improvement or optimization.

8. Continuous Improvement Strategies:

- Feedback Mechanisms: Solicits feedback from partners, customers, and internal stakeholders to identify opportunities for innovation and enhancement.

- Optimization Efforts: Iteratively adjusts strategies, refines tactics, and implements best practices based on performance insights and market feedback.

Software Company Channel Marketing Program:

- **Resources Needed:**

  o A dedicated Channel Manager to oversee partner relationships and program execution.

  o Marketing team to develop co-marketing materials, digital campaigns, and sales enablement resources.

  o CRM system to manage partner interactions, track leads, and monitor performance metrics.

  o Budget allocation for partner incentives, co-op funds, and promotional activities.

  o Training programs, technical support, and documentation to educate partners on software solutions.

  o Legal support to draft partnership agreements, ensure compliance with industry regulations and protect intellectual property.

Creating and managing a channel marketing program requires a strategic alignment of resources, including human expertise, financial investments, technology tools, training programs, marketing collateral, legal support, and performance measurement mechanisms. By leveraging these resources effectively, businesses can establish strong partnerships, optimize distribution channels, and drive growth through collaborative marketing efforts with channel partners.

Best Practices for Channel Marketing Program Management:

- Transparency and Trust: Foster a transparent and trusting relationship with channel partners by sharing information, insights, and market trends.

- Flexibility and Adaptability: Stay agile and adaptable to changing market conditions, customer preferences, and competitive dynamics.

- Incentive and Recognition: Recognize and reward top-performing partners with incentives, bonuses, or special rewards to incentivize sales performance and loyalty.

- Compliance and Governance: Ensure partners adhere to brand guidelines, pricing policies, and regulatory requirements to maintain brand integrity and legal compliance.

Example of Effective Channel Marketing Program Management:

Software Company Example:

- Strategy: A software company partners with IT service providers and consultants to promote a new cloud-based software solution.

- Execution: Provides comprehensive training on product features, offers co-branded marketing materials, and incentivizes partners based on sales milestones.

- Result: Achieves widespread adoption of the software across various industries, expands market reach, and increases revenue through effective channel management.

Successful channel marketing program management requires strategic planning, proactive communication, collaborative partnerships, and continuous evaluation to drive mutual growth and achieve business objectives effectively. By fostering strong relationships and aligning strategies with partners, businesses can optimize channel performance, maximize ROI, and sustain long-term success in competitive markets.

CHAPTER 14
Affiliate and Partner Marketing For Business

Affiliate marketing is a performance-based marketing strategy where businesses (known as merchants or advertisers) partner with individuals or other businesses (known as affiliates or publishers) to promote their products or services in exchange for a commission on sales or leads generated through the affiliate's marketing efforts. It's a popular and effective way for businesses to expand their reach, increase sales, and drive customer acquisition without upfront costs or extensive marketing investments. Here's a detailed explanation of affiliate marketing and its benefits for businesses:

How Affiliate Marketing Works:

1. **Parties Involved:**

   o Merchant/Advertiser: The business that owns the product or service being promoted.

   o Affiliate/Publisher: The individual or entity that promotes the merchant's products or services to their audience.

2. **Process:**

   o Affiliate Promotion: Affiliates promote the merchant's products through various channels such as websites, blogs, social media, email newsletters, or paid advertising.

o Tracking Links: Affiliates use unique tracking links (affiliate links) provided by the merchant to track referrals and sales.

o Conversion Tracking: When a customer clicks on the affiliate link and makes a purchase or performs a desired action (like signing up for a

o newsletter), the affiliate earns a commission based on predefined terms (e.g., percentage of sale or fixed amount per lead).

3. **Commission Models:**

o Pay-per-Sale (PPS): Affiliates earn a commission when their referral results in a sale of the merchant's product or service.

o Pay-per-Lead (PPL): Affiliates earn a commission for each qualified lead they generate for the merchant, such as filling out a contact form or signing up for a trial.

4. **Affiliate Networks:**

o Many merchants use affiliate networks (e.g., Amazon Associates, ShareASale, CJ Affiliate) to manage affiliate programs efficiently. These networks provide a platform for merchants to connect with potential affiliates and manage tracking, payments, and reporting.

Benefits of Affiliate Marketing for Businesses:

1. **Expanded Reach and Market Penetration:**

o Affiliates leverage their own platforms and audiences to promote products, reaching new and diverse customer segments that the merchant may not have accessed otherwise.

o Tap into niche markets and specific demographics through affiliates with targeted content and loyal followings.

2. **Cost-Effective Marketing:**

o Performance-based model: Businesses only pay affiliates when they deliver results (sales or leads), making it a cost-effective marketing strategy.

o Low upfront costs: Minimal investment in advertising or marketing campaigns compared to traditional methods like paid search or display advertising.

3. **Scalability and Growth:**

o Scale quickly: Affiliates can drive significant traffic and sales volume, allowing businesses to scale their operations without proportional increases in marketing spend.

o Enter new markets: Expand geographically or enter new market segments through affiliates with established local or global reach.

4. **Improved SEO and Brand Visibility:**

o Increase website traffic: Affiliates' promotional efforts can drive inbound links and referrals, boosting the merchant's SEO efforts and organic search rankings.

o Enhanced brand visibility: Exposure on multiple platforms and channels increases brand awareness and credibility among potential customers.

5. **Performance Tracking and ROI Measurement:**

   o Trackable results: Advanced tracking tools and analytics provide insights into affiliate performance, allowing businesses to measure ROI accurately.

   o Optimize campaigns: Analyze data to identify top-performing affiliates, optimize marketing strategies, and allocate resources effectively.

6. **Partnership and Relationship Building:**

   o Collaborative partnerships: Build mutually beneficial relationships with affiliates who become advocates for the brand, fostering long-term loyalty and trust.

   o Diversified marketing efforts: Combine strengths and resources with affiliates to create innovative marketing campaigns and promotions.

Example of Affiliate Marketing for an E-commerce Company:

- Objective: An online retailer wants to increase sales of its fashion products.

- Strategy: Partners with fashion bloggers and influencers who have a strong online presence and an engaged audience interested in fashion trends.

- Execution: Provides affiliates with unique tracking links and promotional materials (e.g., discount codes and banners) to share with their followers.

- Result: Affiliates drive traffic to the retailer's website, resulting in increased sales. The retailer pays affiliates a commission for each sale generated through their referrals, achieving a positive ROI and expanding brand reach.

Example of Affiliate Marketing for a Tech Startup:

- Objective: A tech startup launches an affiliate program to increase sales of its software solutions.

- Execution: Partners with industry influencers, bloggers, and tech websites as affiliates.

- Resources: Provides affiliates with high-converting landing pages, promotional discounts, and personalized affiliate support.

- Result: Achieves significant sales growth, expands market reach, and builds brand credibility through strategic affiliate partnerships.

What is Required to Create and Manage an Affiliate Marketing Program

Creating and managing an affiliate marketing program requires careful planning, execution, and ongoing management to ensure its success. Here are the key steps and components needed to establish and effectively manage an affiliate marketing program:

1. Define Program Objectives:

- Goals: Clearly outline the objectives of your affiliate marketing program, such as increasing sales, expanding market reach, or driving lead generation.

- Target Audience: Identify the specific customer segments or demographics you aim to reach through affiliate partnerships.

2. Recruit and Select Affiliates:

- Profile Ideal Affiliates: Identify potential affiliates who align with your brand values, target audience, and marketing objectives.

- Recruitment Strategies: Reach out to affiliates through networks, social media, industry forums, or direct outreach. Highlight the benefits of partnering with your program.

4. Develop Affiliate Program Policies:

- Commission Structure: Define commission rates (e.g., percentage of sale, fixed amount per lead) and payment terms for affiliates.

- Terms and Conditions: Establish guidelines on promotional methods, brand use, compliance with regulations, and dispute resolution.

- Affiliate Agreement: Draft a formal agreement outlining responsibilities, expectations, and legal terms for affiliates to adhere to.

5. Create Marketing Collateral and Tools:

- Promotional Materials: Provide affiliates with banners, text links, product images, and promotional content to use in their marketing efforts.

- Tracking Links: Generate unique affiliate tracking links for each partner to track referrals, sales, and conversions accurately.

6. Offer Training and Support:

- Onboarding Program: Provide comprehensive training sessions or resources to educate affiliates about your products/services, brand guidelines, and promotional strategies.

- Support Channels: Establish communication channels (e.g., email, chat, forums) for affiliates to receive assistance, ask questions, and access support resources.

7. Compliance and Legal Considerations:

- Regulatory Compliance: Ensure compliance with local and international laws, data protection regulations (e.g., GDPR), and industry standards in your affiliate marketing practices.
- Brand Protection: Monitor affiliates' promotional activities to maintain brand integrity and enforce compliance with brand guidelines.

Creating and managing an affiliate marketing program requires strategic planning, effective recruitment, robust program infrastructure, ongoing support, and continuous optimization to drive affiliate performance, expand market reach, and achieve business objectives effectively. By investing in the right resources and implementing best practices, businesses can leverage affiliate partnerships to enhance brand visibility, increase sales revenue, and sustain long-term growth in competitive markets.

Best Practice To Find and Recruit The Best Affiliate Partners

Finding and recruiting the best affiliate partners for your marketing program is crucial for driving quality traffic, increasing conversions, and, ultimately, growing your business. Here's a detailed guide on how to find and recruit top-performing affiliates:

1. Define Your Ideal Affiliate Profile:

- Target Audience: Identify the specific demographics, interests, and behaviors of your target customers. Look for affiliates whose audience closely matches these characteristics.

- Relevance: Ensure that potential affiliates align with your industry, niche, and product/service offerings to ensure relevance in their promotional efforts.

2. Utilize Affiliate Networks and Direct Outreach:

- Affiliate Networks: Join reputable affiliate networks such as ShareASale, CJ Affiliate, or Rakuten Affiliate Network. These platforms provide access to a large pool of affiliates across various industries.

- Direct Outreach: Research and approach potential affiliates directly through their websites, blogs, social media channels, or industry events. Personalized outreach can often yield better results.

3. Evaluate Potential Affiliates:

- Traffic and Audience Size: Assess the affiliate's website traffic, social media following, email list size, and engagement metrics (likes, comments, shares).

- Content Quality: Review the quality of their content, including blog posts, videos, and social media updates. Ensure that their content aligns with your brand values and messaging.

- SEO Performance: Check their search engine rankings, domain authority, and relevance of keywords to gauge their ability to drive organic traffic.

4. Review Affiliate Reputation and Performance:

- Check Reviews and Testimonials: Look for reviews or testimonials from merchants who have worked with the affiliate in the past. Positive feedback indicates reliability and effectiveness.

- Performance Metrics: Analyze their performance data, including conversion rates, average order value (AOV), and return on investment (ROI) from previous affiliate partnerships.

5. Engage in Relationship Building:

- Personalized Outreach: Reach out to potential affiliates with a personalized email or message highlighting why your affiliate program is a good fit for them.

- Offer Value Proposition: Clearly articulate the benefits of partnering with your brand, such as competitive commission rates, exclusive offers, or access to new products/services.

- Build Trust: Establish trust and credibility by demonstrating your brand's integrity, reliability, and commitment to supporting affiliates.

6. Provide Affiliate Resources and Support:

- Marketing Collateral: Offer affiliates ready-to-use marketing materials such as banners, text links, product images, and promotional content.

- Training and Guidance: Provide comprehensive onboarding materials, webinars, or one-on-one training sessions to educate affiliates about your products/services and promotional strategies.

- Dedicated Support: Assign a point of contact or support team to address affiliates' inquiries, provide assistance, and troubleshoot issues promptly.

7. Negotiate Terms and Agreement:

- Commission Structure: Define clear commission rates, payment terms (e.g., frequency and method), and performance incentives based on mutual agreement.

- Contractual Agreement: Draft a formal affiliate agreement outlining roles, responsibilities, promotional guidelines, brand usage policies, and termination clauses.

8. Monitor and Optimize Performance:

- Tracking and Analytics: Use affiliate tracking software or platform analytics to monitor performance metrics in real-time.

- Performance Reviews: Conduct regular performance reviews to assess affiliate effectiveness, identify top performers, and optimize marketing strategies accordingly.

- Feedback Loop: Solicit feedback from affiliates to understand their challenges, gather insights for improvement, and strengthen the partnership over time.

Finding and recruiting the best affiliate partners involves strategic research, personalized outreach, relationship building, and ongoing support. By aligning with affiliates who share your target audience and brand values, providing valuable resources, and optimizing performance, businesses can leverage affiliate partnerships effectively to achieve marketing objectives and drive sustainable growth.

Affiliate marketing offers businesses a cost-effective, scalable, and performance-driven approach to reach new customers, increase sales, and enhance brand visibility through strategic partnerships with affiliates. By leveraging the influence and reach of affiliates, businesses can maximize marketing efforts, drive revenue growth, and achieve sustainable business success in competitive markets.

CHAPTER 15
Market Research in the Digital World

The Need for Market Research: Driving Growth and Success

In today's dynamic business environment, the ability to understand and respond to customer needs, market trends, and competitive landscapes is crucial for sustained growth and success. For growing businesses, this understanding often begins with comprehensive and insightful market research. Let's explore why investing in better market research can be a game-changer for your business's growth trajectory.

Understanding Customer Needs and Preferences

Market research serves as a compass, guiding businesses to navigate the complex landscape of customer preferences and behaviors. By conducting thorough research, businesses can uncover invaluable insights into what drives their customers' purchasing decisions, their pain points, and the features they value most in products or services. This understanding allows businesses to tailor their offerings more precisely, increasing customer satisfaction and loyalty.

Identifying Market Opportunities and Trends

Beyond understanding current customers, market research helps businesses identify emerging opportunities and trends. Whether it's spotting gaps in the market that competitors have overlooked or predicting shifts in consumer behavior, robust research equips businesses with the foresight needed to capitalize on new opportunities swiftly. This proactive approach not only fosters innovation but also positions the business ahead of competitors in adapting to changing market dynamics.

Validating Business Strategies and Decisions

Every strategic decision—from launching a new product to entering a new market—should be informed by data. Market research provides the empirical foundation needed to validate these decisions. By testing hypotheses and gathering feedback from target audiences, businesses can mitigate risks and ensure their strategies align with market demand and customer expectations. This validation process is essential for optimizing resource allocation and maximizing return on investment (ROI).

Enhancing Marketing Effectiveness

Effective marketing hinges on a deep understanding of the target audience. Market research enables businesses to craft targeted marketing campaigns that resonate with specific customer segments. By identifying the most effective communication channels, messaging tactics, and promotional strategies, businesses can optimize their marketing efforts to drive engagement, conversion, and brand loyalty. This precision in marketing not only boosts campaign effectiveness but also optimizes marketing spend.

Improving Competitive Positioning

In today's competitive landscape, businesses must differentiate themselves effectively. Market research provides insights into competitors' strengths and weaknesses, allowing businesses to identify opportunities for differentiation. By benchmarking against industry leaders and understanding market perceptions, businesses can refine their value propositions, enhance their competitive positioning, and carve out a distinct market niche.

Supporting Long-term Business Planning

Market research is not just about immediate gains; it's about laying the groundwork for sustainable growth. By continuously monitoring market trends, consumer preferences, and industry developments, businesses can adapt their long-term strategies to stay ahead of the curve. This strategic foresight enables businesses to anticipate challenges, seize growth opportunities, and maintain agility in an ever-evolving marketplace.

Investing in Your Business's Future

In conclusion, better market research isn't just a luxury for businesses—it's a strategic imperative. By investing in robust research methodologies, businesses can gain a deeper understanding of their customers, identify growth opportunities, validate business strategies, enhance marketing effectiveness, and improve competitive positioning. This proactive approach not only mitigates risks but also accelerates growth by aligning business decisions with market realities. As your business continues to evolve and expand, embracing the power of market research will be instrumental in achieving sustainable success in the competitive landscape.

Ready to take your business to the next level? Start with better market research—it's the compass that guides you toward growth, innovation, and lasting success.

The primary goal of market research is to provide actionable insights that businesses can use to make informed decisions about their products, services, marketing strategies, and overall business operations. Here's an overview of what market research entails and its significance for businesses:

1. **Understanding Customer Needs and Preferences:**

   o Demographic Analysis: Identifying key demographic characteristics such as age, gender, income, education, and lifestyle of target customers.

   o Psychographic Profiling: Understanding customers' motivations, values, interests, and purchasing behaviors.

   o Customer Feedback: Gathering direct feedback through surveys, interviews, focus groups, or social media interactions to uncover preferences, satisfaction levels, and pain points.

2. **Analyzing Market Trends and Conditions:**

   o Industry Analysis: Assessing the overall size, growth rate, and dynamics of the industry relevant to the business.

   o Competitive Analysis: Studying competitors' offerings, pricing strategies, market positioning, strengths, weaknesses, and market share.

   o Trend Identification: Monitoring emerging trends, technological advancements, regulatory changes, and shifts in consumer behavior that could impact the market.

3. **Evaluating Market Potential and Opportunities:**

   o Market Segmentation: Dividing the market into distinct segments based on criteria such as demographics, behavior, needs, or geographic location.

o Target Market Identification: Selecting specific segments that represent the best opportunities for the business based on attractiveness, size, growth potential, and competitive landscape.

o Opportunity Assessment: Identifying unmet needs, gaps in the market, or underserved customer segments that present opportunities for innovation and growth.

4. **Assessing Product or Service Viability:**

o Concept Testing: Evaluating consumer interest, acceptance, and perceived value of new product or service concepts before launch.

o Product Testing: Conducting beta testing, prototypes, or pilot studies to gather feedback on product performance, usability, and satisfaction.

o Price Sensitivity Analysis: Determining optimal pricing strategies through surveys or conjoint analysis to understand how pricing affects consumer purchase decisions.

5. **Supporting Marketing and Business Strategy:**

o Marketing Effectiveness: Measuring the effectiveness of marketing campaigns, advertising messages, and promotional activities in reaching and resonating with target audiences.

o Brand Perception: Assessing brand awareness, perception, and equity among consumers relative to competitors.

o Channel and Distribution Analysis: Evaluating the effectiveness of distribution channels and identifying opportunities to optimize reach and efficiency.

Significance of Market Research for Businesses:

- Risk Mitigation: Reducing risks associated with launching new products, entering new markets, or making strategic business decisions by basing them on empirical data and insights.

- Strategic Decision-Making: Providing a foundation for strategic planning, resource allocation, and investment decisions aligned with market opportunities and customer needs.

- Competitive Advantage: Gaining a competitive edge by understanding market dynamics, anticipating trends, and responding proactively to changes in consumer preferences and competitive activities.

- Customer-Centric Approach: Enabling businesses to tailor products, services, and marketing efforts to meet the specific needs and preferences of target customers, enhancing customer satisfaction and loyalty.

- Business Growth: Identifying growth opportunities, expanding market presence, and optimizing resource utilization to drive revenue growth and profitability over the long term.

Market Research In Today's Digital World and the Internet

Market research has undergone significant transformation in today's digital-first world, driven by technological advancements, changing consumer behaviors, and the availability of vast amounts of data. Here are key ways in which market research has evolved:

1. Access to Real-Time Data:

- Digital Analytics: Businesses can now gather real-time data from various digital platforms such as websites, social media, mobile apps, and e-commerce transactions. This allows for continuous monitoring of consumer behavior, trends, and interactions with brands.

2. Big Data and Predictive Analytics:

- Data Integration: Integration of big data sources enables comprehensive analysis of large volumes of structured and unstructured data, providing deeper insights into customer preferences, market trends, and competitive dynamics.

- Predictive Models: Advanced analytics techniques like machine learning and AI are used to develop predictive models for forecasting market trends, customer behavior, and future demand patterns.

3. Increased Personalization:

- Customer Segmentation: Enhanced segmentation capabilities allow businesses to create more precise customer profiles based on behavior, preferences, and purchase history.

- Targeted Marketing: Personalized marketing strategies leverage data-driven insights to deliver relevant content, offers, and experiences tailored to individual customer segments.

4. Digital Tools and Automation:

- Survey Tools: Online survey platforms streamline the process of gathering consumer feedback and insights through customizable surveys, polls, and feedback forms.

- Social Listening: Monitoring social media platforms for mentions, sentiment analysis, and trends provides real-time feedback on brand perception and consumer sentiment.

5. Global Reach and Accessibility:

- Remote Research: Conducting market research remotely has become feasible through online surveys, virtual focus groups, and digital ethnography, enabling access to global markets without geographical constraints.

- Audience Reach: Digital platforms facilitate reaching diverse audiences across different demographics, geographies, and cultural backgrounds for more representative research samples.

6. Customer Engagement and Feedback:

- Interactive Platforms: Social media and community forums enable direct engagement with customers, facilitating ongoing conversations, feedback collection, and sentiment analysis.

- User-Generated Content: Monitoring user-generated content provides authentic insights into customer experiences, opinions, and product preferences.

7. Agility and Iterative Learning:

- Iterative Testing: Agile methodologies allow for rapid testing and iteration of marketing campaigns, product features, and business strategies based on real-time feedback and performance data.

- Continuous Improvement: Continuous monitoring and analysis of digital metrics enable businesses to refine strategies, optimize customer experiences, and respond quickly to market changes.

8. Ethical Considerations and Data Privacy:

- **Compliance:** Adherence to data privacy regulations (e.g., GDPR, CCPA) and ethical guidelines in data collection, storage, and usage to protect consumer privacy and build trust.

Impact on Businesses:

- Competitive Advantage: Businesses that leverage digital-first market research strategies gain a competitive edge by making data-driven decisions, anticipating market trends, and responding swiftly to consumer preferences.

- Innovation: Access to real-time insights and customer feedback fuels innovation in product development, marketing strategies, and service delivery.

- Customer-Centricity: Enhanced understanding of customer needs and behaviors enables businesses to tailor offerings and experiences that resonate with their target audience, driving customer satisfaction and loyalty.

Market research in today's digital-first world is characterized by its reliance on real-time data, advanced analytics, personalized approaches, and enhanced customer engagement. By harnessing digital technologies and data-driven insights, businesses can adapt more effectively to dynamic market conditions, foster innovation, and achieve sustainable growth in a rapidly evolving business environment.

When to Consider a Do-It-Yourself Market Research:

- Budget Constraints: Small businesses or startups with limited budgets may opt for DIY research using available tools and resources.

- Immediate Insights: When quick feedback or preliminary data is needed, DIY methods like online surveys or social media monitoring can provide timely insights.

- In-House Expertise: Businesses with in-house research capabilities and experienced analysts may prefer to conduct research internally to maintain control and confidentiality.

Best Practice for Doing Your Own Market Research

Conducting DIY (Do-It-Yourself) market research can be a cost-effective way for businesses, especially startups and small enterprises, to gather valuable insights without relying on extensive external resources. Here's a best practice guide for conducting DIY market research:

1. Define Your Objectives and Scope:

- Clear Goals: Determine what specific information you need to gather, such as understanding customer needs, evaluating market demand, or assessing competitors.

- Scope: Define the scope of your research, including target audience demographics, geographical focus, and the depth of insights required.

2. **Utilize Available Secondary Research:**

- Industry Reports: Access online databases, industry associations, and government publications for free or low-cost reports on market trends, industry forecasts, and consumer behavior.

- Competitor Analysis: Review competitors' websites, social media channels, pricing strategies, and product/service offerings to identify gaps and competitive positioning.

3. **Conduct Online Surveys and Questionnaires:**

- Survey Tools: Use online survey platforms like SurveyMonkey, Google Forms, or Typeform to create and distribute surveys to your target audience.

- Targeted Questions: Design clear, concise, and relevant questions to gather feedback on customer preferences, satisfaction levels, and purchase intentions.

4. **Engage in Social Listening and Online Communities:**

- Social Media Monitoring: Monitor conversations, mentions, and hashtags related to your industry, brand, or products/services on social media platforms to gauge sentiment and trends.

- Online Forums and Groups: Participate in relevant online forums, LinkedIn groups, or Reddit threads to observe discussions, gather insights, and engage with potential customers.

5. Direct Customer Feedback and Interviews:

- Customer Surveys: Include feedback forms or surveys on your website, post-purchase emails, or checkout pages to gather immediate customer feedback and suggestions.

- Interviews: Conduct phone or email interviews with existing customers, prospects, or industry experts to delve deeper into specific topics and gain qualitative insights.

6. Website and Analytics Review:

- Google Analytics: Analyze website traffic, user behavior, conversion rates, and demographics to understand visitor preferences, popular content, and areas for improvement.

- Heatmaps and Click Tracking: Use tools like Hotjar or Crazy Egg to visualize user interactions on your website, identifying where visitors click, scroll, or drop off.

7. Evaluate Pricing and Competitive Positioning:

- Price Sensitivity: Test different pricing strategies through A/B testing or surveys to understand how price impacts purchase decisions.

- Competitor Pricing: Compare your pricing with competitors to determine your market positioning and identify opportunities for pricing adjustments.

8. SWOT Analysis and Market Segmentation:

- SWOT Analysis: Evaluate your business's strengths, weaknesses, opportunities, and threats to understand internal capabilities and external market dynamics.

- Segmentation: Segment your target market based on demographics, psychographics, or behavioral traits to tailor marketing strategies and product offerings effectively.

9. Data Analysis and Reporting:

- Compile Findings: Organize and analyze collected data using spreadsheets, charts, or dashboards to identify patterns, trends, and actionable insights.

- Report Insights: Prepare a concise summary or report outlining key findings, recommendations, and strategic implications for decision-making.

10. Iterate and Improve:

- Continuous Feedback: Incorporate feedback loops into your research process to continuously refine your understanding of market dynamics and customer needs.

- Iterative Approach: Iterate your research methods based on initial findings, testing new hypotheses, and adapting strategies to optimize outcomes over time.

Online Retail Startup DIY Market Research:

- Objective: An online retail startup aims to validate market demand for eco-friendly home products.

- Approach: Conducts online surveys targeting environmentally conscious consumers, analyzes competitor pricing and product offerings, and engages with online communities to gather feedback.

- Outcome: Identifies strong interest in sustainable home products, refines product assortment based on customer preferences, and establishes competitive pricing strategies.

By following these best practices for DIY market research, businesses can effectively gather valuable insights, validate assumptions, and make informed decisions to drive growth and competitiveness in their respective markets.

Reasons to Consider a Market Research Firm:

Considering a market research firm can be beneficial for businesses, depending on their specific needs, resources, and objectives. Here are some reasons why you might consider engaging a market research firm:

1. **Expertise and Experience:**

   o Specialized Knowledge: Market research firms bring expertise in research methodologies, data analysis, and interpretation of findings that may not be available in-house.

   o Industry Insights: They often have experience working across various industries and sectors, providing valuable benchmarking and best practices tailored to your business needs.

2. **Access to Advanced Tools and Technologies:**

o Research Tools: Market research firms have access to sophisticated tools, software, and databases for data collection, analysis, and visualization, which can yield more robust and actionable insights.

o Technology Integration: They leverage advanced analytics, predictive modeling, and artificial intelligence to uncover hidden trends, patterns, and opportunities in large datasets.

3. **Objectivity and Impartiality:**

o Neutral Perspective: External market researchers provide an unbiased and impartial view of market conditions, customer perceptions, and competitive landscapes.

o Independent Validation: Their findings can validate internal assumptions and mitigate biases that may influence internal research conducted by company stakeholders.

4. **Efficiency and Resource Optimization:**

o Time Savings: Outsourcing market research tasks allows internal teams to focus on core business activities and strategic initiatives without the overhead of managing research projects.

o Cost-Effectiveness: While initial costs may be higher, leveraging external expertise can result in more efficient research execution, faster turnaround times, and higher-quality insights.

5. **Broadened Scope and Global Reach:**

o Geographical Reach: Market research firms often have global reach and capabilities to conduct research across multiple markets, languages, and cultural contexts.

o Comprehensive Insights: They can provide insights into international market trends, regulatory landscapes, and consumer behaviors that may impact your business expansion strategies.

6. **Strategic Guidance and Actionable Recommendations:**

o Strategic Insights: Firms offer strategic guidance based on research findings, helping businesses make informed decisions, mitigate risks, and capitalize on market opportunities.

o Actionable Recommendations: They deliver actionable recommendations for product development, marketing strategies, pricing optimization, and customer experience improvements based on data-driven insights.

Engaging a market research firm can be advantageous for businesses seeking specialized expertise, advanced research capabilities, and unbiased insights to support strategic decision-making and drive competitive advantage in dynamic market environments. Assessing your specific needs, budgetary considerations, and desired outcomes will help determine whether outsourcing to a market research firm aligns with your business objectives.

Market research is essential for businesses seeking to understand their market environment, make informed decisions, and stay competitive in dynamic and evolving market landscapes. By leveraging market insights effectively, businesses can enhance their strategic positioning, foster innovation, and achieve sustainable business success.

CHAPTER 16
How To Build Your Customer Personas

In today's competitive marketplace, understanding your customers isn't just beneficial—it's essential for business success. One of the most effective tools for gaining insights into your target audience is creating personas. Personas are detailed representations of your ideal customers based on research and data. They help businesses visualize and understand the diverse needs, behaviors, and preferences of their customer base. Let's explore why creating personas is crucial for businesses aiming to thrive in the digital age.

Targeted Marketing and Personalization

Creating personas allows businesses to tailor their marketing efforts with precision. By defining specific demographics, psychographics, and purchasing behaviors of different customer segments, personas enable targeted marketing strategies. This personalized approach ensures that marketing messages resonate more effectively with different customer groups, leading to higher engagement and conversion rates.

Insightful Customer Understanding

Personas provide businesses with a deeper understanding of their customers' motivations, goals, challenges, and pain points. Through research methods such as surveys, interviews, and data analytics, businesses can gather valuable insights that inform product development, service enhancements, and overall customer experience strategies. This customer-centric approach fosters empathy and strengthens relationships with customers by addressing their specific needs and preferences.

Strategic Decision-Making

Personas serve as valuable tools for strategic decision-making across various departments within an organization. From product managers and marketers to sales teams and customer service representatives, personas guide decisions related to product features, pricing strategies, channel selection, and messaging tactics. By aligning business strategies with the expectations and behaviors of different personas, businesses can optimize resource allocation and maximize ROI.

Competitive Advantage

Understanding your customers better than your competitors gives your business a competitive edge. Personas help businesses identify market gaps, differentiate their offerings, and develop unique value propositions that resonate with target audiences. By continuously refining personas based on market research and feedback, businesses can stay agile and responsive to changing market dynamics, maintaining their competitive advantage over time.

Improved Customer Engagement and Satisfaction

Personalized customer experiences lead to higher levels of engagement and satisfaction. By leveraging personas to deliver relevant content, personalized recommendations, and targeted promotions, businesses enhance the overall customer journey. This customer-centric approach not only increases retention rates but also cultivates brand loyalty as customers feel understood and valued by the business.

Efficient Use of Resources

By focusing marketing efforts on specific personas, businesses can optimize their marketing budgets and resources effectively. Rather than adopting a one-size-fits-all approach, personas enable businesses to prioritize initiatives that are most likely to resonate with their target audience. This strategic allocation of resources ensures that marketing campaigns are more cost-effective and yield better results.

Continuous Improvement and Innovation

Personas facilitate continuous improvement and innovation by providing a structured framework for gathering feedback and iterating on products and services. By listening to the voice of the customer through persona insights, businesses can identify opportunities for innovation, anticipate market trends, and proactively address evolving customer needs. This iterative process fosters a culture of innovation and agility within the organization, driving long-term growth and sustainability.

Embracing Personas for Business Success

Creating personas is not just about understanding who your customers are—it's about anticipating what they need and delivering exceptional experiences that exceed their expectations. By investing in persona development and integrating persona insights into business strategies, organizations can achieve greater marketing effectiveness, customer satisfaction, and competitive advantage in today's dynamic marketplace. As businesses continue to evolve, personas remain invaluable tools for driving growth, fostering innovation, and building lasting customer relationships.

Here are several reasons why businesses should invest in creating personas:

1. Targeted Marketing and Messaging:

- Personalization: Personas help tailor marketing messages and content to resonate with specific customer segments, increasing relevance and engagement.

- Precision: By understanding the unique challenges, goals, and pain points of each persona, businesses can craft compelling campaigns that address their audience's needs effectively.

2. Improved Customer Understanding:

- Empathy: Personas humanize data by creating fictional characters that represent real customers, fostering empathy and a deeper understanding of their behaviors and decision-making processes.

- Insight Generation: Insights derived from personas guide product development, service offerings, and customer experience strategies, ensuring they align closely with customer expectations.

3. Enhanced Customer Experience:

- Customization: Businesses can personalize interactions across various touchpoints based on persona insights, providing a seamless and satisfying customer experience.

- Retention: Meeting specific needs identified through personas can enhance customer satisfaction and loyalty and reduce churn rates.

4. Strategic Decision-Making:

- **Focus:** Personas help prioritize marketing efforts and resource allocation by identifying high-value customer segments and their potential impact on business growth.

- **Differentiation:** Businesses can use personas to differentiate their offerings in competitive markets by highlighting unique value propositions that resonate with specific customer groups.

5. Product and Service Development:

- **Innovation:** Understanding persona preferences and pain points informs product/service improvements and innovation, ensuring offerings meet market demand.

- **Validation:** Personas validate assumptions about customer behavior through data-driven insights, minimizing risks associated with new product launches or business initiatives.

6. Efficient Resource Allocation:

- **Cost-Effectiveness:** Targeting personas with the highest ROI potential optimizes marketing spend, improves campaign performance, and maximizes the efficiency of sales and marketing efforts.

- **Focus:** Aligning strategies with persona needs prevents wasted resources on broad, generic approaches that may not resonate with specific customer segments.

7. Competitive Advantage:

- **Market Positioning:** Businesses can use personas to refine their positioning in the market, identifying unique selling propositions that set them apart from competitors.

- **Adaptability:** Persona insights enable businesses to adapt quickly to market changes and trends, staying relevant and responsive to evolving customer preferences.

8. Cross-Functional Alignment:

- **Internal Alignment:** Personas facilitate collaboration and alignment across departments (marketing, sales, product development, customer service) by providing a unified understanding of customer priorities and expectations.

- **Consistency:** Ensures consistent messaging and customer interactions across all organizational touchpoints, reinforcing brand identity and customer trust.

Creating customer personas empowers businesses to connect more deeply with their target audience, drive customer-centric strategies, foster innovation, and gain a competitive edge in today's dynamic marketplace. By investing in persona development, businesses can build stronger customer relationships, improve business outcomes, and achieve sustainable growth over the long term.

Here's how you can create customer personas, along with three detailed examples:

1. Gather Data and Insights:

- **Demographics:** Age, gender, income, education level, marital status, occupation, and family size.

- **Psychographics:** Interests, hobbies, lifestyle, values, attitudes, and personality traits.

- **Behavioral Insights:** Purchasing behaviors, buying motivations, decision-making criteria, preferred channels, and content consumption habits.

- **Challenges and Pain Points.:** Common issues, problems, and obstacles faced in relation to your products or services.

2. **Segmentation and Grouping:**

- **Identify Patterns:** Group customers into segments based on similarities in demographics, behaviors, or needs.

- **Prioritize Segments:** Focus on segments that represent the highest value or growth potential for your business.

3. **Create Persona Profiles:**

- **Name and Title:** Give each persona a representative name and job title to humanize them.

- **Demographic Details:** Include age, gender, location, income, education, and family status.

- **Background:** Describe their career, industry, job responsibilities, and professional aspirations.

- **Goals and Motivations:** Outline their primary goals, both personal and professional, related to your products or services.

- **Challenges and Pain Points:** Highlight the obstacles they face that your offerings can address.

- **Preferred Channels:** Specify their preferred communication channels, media consumption habits, and sources of information.

- **Buying Behavior:** Detail their decision-making process, factors influencing purchases, and objections they might raise.

4. Visual Representation:

- **Persona Image:** Use stock photos or create visual representations to accompany each persona profile, adding a visual element to aid in understanding and empathy.

Example Customer Persona 1: "Tech-Savvy Millennial Mark"

- **Name:** Mark Johnson

- **Age:** 28

- **Location:** Urban area, USA

- **Occupation:** Digital Marketing Specialist

- **Income:** $60,000 annually

- **Education:** Bachelor's degree in Marketing

- **Family Status:** Single

- **Background:** Mark is passionate about digital trends and enjoys experimenting with new technologies. He works in a fast-paced agency environment and values efficiency and innovation.

- **Goals and Motivations:** Mark seeks tools and solutions that streamline workflows, enhance creativity, and improve campaign performance. He aspires to advance in his career and stay ahead of industry trends.

- **Challenges:** Managing multiple client accounts, staying updated with evolving digital platforms, and proving ROI on marketing investments.

- **Preferred Channels:** Active on LinkedIn for professional networking, follows industry blogs and podcasts, prefers webinars and online courses for skill development.

- **Buying Behavior:** Makes informed decisions based on data and analytics, values peer recommendations and expert reviews, and seeks tools with user-friendly interfaces and robust customer support.

Example Customer Persona 2: "Family-Oriented Parent Pam"

- **Name:** Pamela Martinez

- **Age:** 35

- **Location:** Suburban area, Canada

- **Occupation:** Stay-at-home parent, part-time freelance writer

- **Income:** Household income $80,000 annually

- **Education:** College graduate

- **Family Status:** Married with two children (ages 7 and 10)

- **Background:** Pamela is dedicated to her family's well-being and enjoys writing in her spare time. She values products and services that simplify her daily routines and enhance family experiences.

- **Goals and Motivations:** Pamela seeks affordable solutions that cater to her family's needs, such as educational tools, home organization products, and family-friendly activities.

- **Challenges:** Balancing work and family responsibilities, managing household finances, finding reliable childcare options, and ensuring her children's educational and social development.

- **Preferred Channels:** Actively engages in parenting forums and social media groups, follows parenting blogs and influencers on Instagram and Pinterest, and trusts recommendations from fellow parents.

- **Buying Behavior:** Makes purchases based on value for money, prioritizes safety and quality, and is influenced by online reviews and recommendations from trusted sources.

Example Customer Persona 3: "Senior Health-Conscious Sarah"

- **Name:** Sarah Thompson

- **Age:** 65

- **Location:** Rural area, UK

- **Occupation:** Retired teacher

- **Income:** Pension income

- **Education:** Master's degree

- **Family Status:** Widowed, with grown children

- **Background:** Sarah enjoys an active lifestyle and prioritizes health and wellness. She spends her retirement volunteering, gardening, and exploring new hobbies.

- **Goals and Motivations:** Sarah seeks products and services that support her physical health, mental well-being, and social interactions. She values convenience and reliability in her purchases.

- **Challenges:** Managing health issues associated with aging, staying connected with family and community, and adapting to technological advancements.

- **Preferred Channels:** Reads health magazines and community newsletters, participates in local senior groups and fitness classes, prefers face-to-face interactions and traditional media.

- **Buying Behavior:** Values personalized customer service, seeks products endorsed by healthcare professionals and makes purchases based on trust and long-term benefits.

Benefits of Using Customer Personas:

- **Targeted Marketing:** Enables personalized messaging and content strategies tailored to specific customer segments.

- **Product Development:** Guides product features, design, and enhancements that resonate with customer needs and preferences.

- **Customer Experience:** Improves customer satisfaction and loyalty by anticipating needs and delivering relevant solutions.

- **Decision-Making:** Informs strategic decisions related to pricing, distribution channels, and market positioning.

- **Competitive Advantage:** Helps differentiate your offerings and attract and retain profitable customer segments.

Best Practices for Building Personas To Support Marketing Campaigns.

Creating and using personas effectively in marketing campaigns involves several best practices to ensure they are actionable, insightful, and impactful. Here are key best practices for creating and utilizing personas in your marketing strategies:

1. Conduct Comprehensive Research:

- **Data Collection:** Gather quantitative and qualitative data from various sources, including customer surveys, interviews, website analytics, social media insights, and CRM data.

- **Market Segmentation:** Identify common patterns and characteristics to group customers into distinct personas based on demographics, behaviors, motivations, and goals.

2. Develop Detailed Persona Profiles:

- **Name and Details:** Give each persona a name and include relevant details such as age, gender, occupation, income level, family status, and educational background.

- **Psychographic Insights:** Describe their interests, values, lifestyle choices, hobbies, attitudes, and personality traits that influence their purchasing decisions.

3. Validate and Refine Personas:

- **Feedback Loops:** Continuously validate personas with feedback from customer interactions, sales data, and market trends to ensure accuracy and relevance.

- **Iterative Approach:** Refine personas over time based on new insights and changes in customer behaviors or market dynamics.

4. Prioritize Key Persona Attributes:

- **Primary Goals and Challenges:** Clearly define each persona's primary goals, motivations, pain points, and challenges they face in relation to your products or services.

- **Buying Behavior:** Understand their decision-making process, preferred channels of communication, and factors influencing their purchasing decisions.

5. Create Persona-Centric Content:

- **Tailored Messaging:** Develop marketing messages and content that speak directly to each persona's needs, interests, and aspirations.

- **Content Formats:** Adapt content formats (blogs, videos, infographics) and tone of voice to resonate with different personas across various stages of the buyer's journey.

6. Map Customer Journeys:

- **Customer Touchpoints:** Map out the typical journey each persona takes from awareness to conversion and beyond, identifying opportunities to engage and influence decision-making.

- **Personalized Experiences:** Deliver personalized experiences at each touchpoint based on persona preferences and behaviors to enhance engagement and satisfaction.

7. Align Sales and Marketing Efforts:

- **Shared Understanding:** Ensure alignment between sales and marketing teams on persona profiles, goals, and strategies to streamline lead nurturing and customer retention efforts.

- **Feedback Integration:** Incorporate sales team feedback on persona effectiveness and adjust marketing tactics accordingly to optimize campaign performance.

8. Measure and Analyze Persona Impact:

- **Performance Metrics:** Define KPIs (Key Performance Indicators) aligned with persona objectives, such as conversion rates, engagement levels, and customer lifetime value.

- **A/B Testing:** Conduct A/B tests to compare the effectiveness of persona-specific campaigns and refine strategies based on data-driven insights.

9. Stay Agile and Adapt:

- **Market Dynamics:** Monitor market trends, competitor activities, and customer feedback to adapt persona strategies and remain agile in responding to evolving customer needs.

- **Continuous Improvement:** Iterate on persona development and campaign strategies based on ongoing learnings and feedback loops to maintain relevance and effectiveness.

10. Educate and Train Teams:

- **Internal Communication:** Educate all team members across departments about persona profiles, their role in customer interactions, and the importance of delivering consistent customer experiences.

- **Training Programs:** Implement training programs to enhance empathy and understanding of personas, ensuring all customer-facing staff can effectively engage and support diverse customer segments.

By implementing these best practices, businesses can create more targeted and effective marketing campaigns that resonate with their audience, drive engagement, and ultimately contribute to business growth and customer loyalty. Personas serve as valuable tools for understanding and connecting with customers on a deeper level, guiding strategic decisions, and optimizing marketing investments for maximum impact.

CHAPTER 17
Managing Events With Digital Marketing Programs

The Power of Event Marketing: Connecting Businesses with Their Audience

In the fast-paced world of digital marketing, where online interactions dominate, event marketing stands out as a powerful strategy for businesses to engage directly with their audience. Whether it's a trade show, conference, seminar, workshop, or virtual event, these gatherings provide unique opportunities for businesses to showcase their products, build relationships, and strengthen their brand presence. Let's delve into what event marketing entails and why it is crucial for businesses aiming to make a lasting impact.

What is Event Marketing

Event marketing refers to the strategy of promoting a brand, product, or service through in-person or virtual events. These events are designed to attract a targeted audience and create meaningful interactions that drive brand awareness, customer engagement, and, ultimately, business growth. Event marketing encompasses a wide range of activities, from hosting exclusive corporate events to participating in industry expos and sponsoring community gatherings.

Industry events play a pivotal role in the growth and success of businesses across various sectors. Whether you're a startup looking to establish a foothold in your industry or a seasoned enterprise aiming to reinforce your market position, actively participating in and supporting industry events can offer numerous benefits. Let's explore why businesses should prioritize and invest in industry events:

Networking Opportunities

One of the most significant advantages of attending industry events is the unparalleled networking opportunities they provide. These events bring together professionals, thought leaders, potential clients, and industry influencers under one roof. Networking allows businesses to:

- **Expand their Network:** Forge new connections and expand their professional network beyond existing contacts.

- **Build Relationships:** Cultivate meaningful relationships with peers, prospects, and partners that can lead to collaborations, referrals, or strategic alliances.

- **Access Industry Insights:** Gain valuable insights into industry trends, market dynamics, and emerging technologies through conversations and discussions with industry experts.

Face-to-Face Interaction and Relationship Building

In an increasingly digital world, face-to-face interactions are more valuable than ever. Events provide businesses with the opportunity to meet prospects, customers, and industry influencers in person. These personal connections help build trust, strengthen relationships, and foster a sense of community around the brand. Direct engagement allows businesses to showcase their expertise, address customer concerns, and demonstrate the value of their products/services in real-time.

Brand Visibility and Recognition

Participating in or hosting events enhances brand visibility and recognition within target markets. By aligning with industry-specific events or hosting branded experiences, businesses can position themselves as thought leaders and innovators in their field. Consistent participation in relevant events reinforces brand presence and reinforces key messaging among attendees, increasing brand recall and differentiation from competitors.

Lead Generation and Sales Opportunities

Events serve as powerful platforms for lead generation and sales conversion. Through targeted pre-event promotions and onsite interactions, businesses can capture qualified leads interested in their offerings. Demonstrations, product launches, and interactive sessions at events allow prospects to experience firsthand the benefits of products/services, making them more likely to convert into paying customers. Post-event follow-ups further nurture leads and facilitate the sales process.

Market Research and Customer Insights

Events provide valuable opportunities for businesses to conduct market research and gather direct feedback from attendees. Surveys, polls, and informal conversations with participants yield insights into market trends, customer preferences, and competitive intelligence. These insights inform product development, marketing strategies, and business decisions, ensuring alignment with customer needs and expectations.

Brand Authority and Thought Leadership

Hosting or participating in industry events positions businesses as authoritative voices within their niche. Speaking engagements, panel discussions, and thought leadership presentations enable businesses to share expertise, industry knowledge, and innovative solutions with a captive audience. Establishing thought leadership enhances brand credibility, attracts media attention, and opens doors to partnership opportunities and collaborations with industry peers.

Community Engagement and Brand Loyalty

Events create opportunities for businesses to engage with their community and foster brand loyalty. By organizing networking events, customer appreciation gatherings, or charity fundraisers, businesses demonstrate their commitment to supporting and connecting with their audience beyond transactional relationships. Positive event experiences leave a lasting impression on attendees, encouraging repeat business and advocacy among satisfied customers.

Professional Development and Learning

Industry events provide continuous learning and professional development opportunities for businesses and their employees. Attendees can:

- **Attend Educational Sessions:** Participate in workshops, panel discussions, and keynote presentations to gain insights into industry best practices, strategies, and future trends.

- **Stay Updated:** Stay abreast of the latest advancements in technology, regulations, and market shifts that impact their business operations.

- **Skill Enhancement:** Acquire new skills, expand knowledge, and refine existing competencies through interactive learning experiences offered at events.

Harnessing the Potential of Event Marketing

Event marketing is not just about hosting gatherings—it's about creating memorable experiences that resonate with attendees and drive business objectives. From building relationships and generating leads to enhancing brand visibility and establishing thought leadership, events play a pivotal role in the marketing mix of businesses seeking to stand out in competitive markets. By strategically integrating event marketing into their overall strategy, businesses can achieve measurable results, foster growth, and cultivate a loyal customer base that continues to thrive.

Managing an Industry Event: A Comprehensive Guide

Managing an industry event requires meticulous planning, seamless execution, and effective follow-up to ensure its success and maximize its impact. Whether you're organizing a trade show, conference, seminar, or networking event, each phase—pre-event, during the event, and post-event—plays a crucial role in delivering a memorable experience for attendees and achieving your business objectives. Let's delve into how to manage an industry event effectively across these three key phases:

Pre-Event Activities

1. **Set Clear Objectives and Goals:**

   o Define the purpose of the event, whether it's lead generation, brand awareness, networking, or education. Establish specific, measurable goals to track success.

2. **Create a Detailed Event Plan:**

- o Develop a comprehensive timeline and checklist outlining tasks such as securing a venue, booking speakers, arranging catering, organizing logistics, and marketing the event.

3. **Identify and Understand Your Audience:**

- o Conduct market research and create attendee personas to tailor your event content, marketing messages, and activities to meet the needs and interests of your target audience.

4. **Promote the Event:**

- o Utilize a multi-channel marketing strategy to promote the event, including email campaigns, social media posts, digital advertising, and partnerships with industry influencers or media outlets.

5. **Manage Registrations and Logistics:**

- o Set up an online registration system and manage attendee communications. Coordinate logistics such as transportation, accommodation (if necessary), and onsite facilities.

6. **Prepare Event Materials and Collaterals:**

- o Design and produce necessary materials such as signage, name badges, promotional materials, presentation slides, and handouts for attendees, speakers, and sponsors.

During the Event

1. **Ensure Smooth Onsite Operations:**

- o Arrive early to oversee setup and ensure everything is in place. Assign staff to manage registration desks, handle inquiries, and troubleshoot any issues that arise.

2. **Engage Attendees and Facilitate Networking:**

o   Encourage attendee interaction through networking sessions, Q&A panels, breakout discussions, and social activities. Foster a welcoming atmosphere conducive to relationship-building.

3. **Coordinate Speakers and Sessions:**

o   Maintain a schedule of sessions and keynote speeches. Ensure speakers are briefed, presentations are queued, and technical equipment is functioning smoothly.

4. **Capture Content and Feedback:**

o   Record sessions (with permission) and collect attendee feedback through surveys or onsite evaluations. Monitor social media for attendee engagement and event mentions.

5. **Support Sponsors and Exhibitors:**

o   Provide sponsors and exhibitors with dedicated support, ensuring they have the resources and visibility promised in their agreements. Facilitate connections between sponsors/exhibitors and attendees.

6. **Handle Unexpected Situations:**

o   Stay adaptable and responsive to unforeseen challenges such as technical glitches, attendee concerns, or schedule changes. Have contingency plans in place to minimize disruptions.

Post-Event Activities

1. **Follow-Up with Attendees:**

   o Send personalized thank-you emails to attendees, speakers, sponsors, and exhibitors. Share event highlights, session recordings, and any additional resources promised during the event.

2. **Evaluate Event Success Against Goals:**

   o Review attendee feedback, survey responses, and key performance metrics (e.g., attendance rate, engagement levels, lead generation). Analyze whether goals were met and identify areas for improvement.

3. **Measure Return on Investment (ROI):**

   o Calculate the ROI based on event expenses versus generated revenue, new leads, partnerships established, or brand exposure gained. Use these insights to justify future event investments.

4. **Debrief and Document Learnings:**

   o Conduct a post-event debrief with your team and key stakeholders to discuss successes, challenges, and lessons learned. Document these insights to inform future event planning and execution.

5. **Nurture Relationships and Follow-Up Leads:**

   o Continue nurturing relationships with leads generated during the event through personalized follow-up communications. Share relevant content and maintain engagement to convert leads into customers.

6. Plan for Future Events:

o Use the insights gathered to refine your event strategy for future initiatives. Incorporate attendee feedback, adjust marketing tactics, and explore new opportunities for growth and expansion.

Managing an industry event requires meticulous planning, proactive communication, and a commitment to delivering value to attendees, sponsors, and stakeholders. By carefully orchestrating pre-event preparations, ensuring seamless execution during the event, and conducting thorough post-event follow-up, businesses can maximize the impact of their events and achieve strategic objectives. Embrace each phase of event management as an opportunity to engage, inspire, and build lasting relationships within your industry.

Maximizing Your Time at Industry Events

Imagine you run a software startup specializing in artificial intelligence solutions for healthcare. You're attending a prominent healthcare technology conference with the goal of networking with potential clients, showcasing your latest product innovations, and establishing thought leadership in the field. Here's how you can strategically maximize your time and resources at the event:

Tradeshow Booth and Presentation

- Strategic Booth Design: Design your booth to be inviting and professional, with clear signage and branding that reflects your company's identity. Incorporate interactive elements like live demos or virtual reality experiences to engage visitors and demonstrate your technology firsthand.

- Schedule Demos and Meetings: Offer pre-scheduled demos of your AI solutions to interested prospects. Use a scheduling tool or appointment-setting system to manage meetings efficiently and maximize face-to-face interactions during the event.

- Host Thought Leadership Sessions: Secure speaking opportunities or panel discussions to showcase your expertise. Prepare insightful presentations on AI trends in healthcare, case studies of successful implementations, or future predictions for the industry.

Networking and Engagement

- Attend Relevant Sessions: Participate in sessions and workshops related to healthcare technology and AI. Take notes, ask questions, and contribute to discussions to demonstrate your industry knowledge and build rapport with fellow attendees.

- Utilize Networking Opportunities: Attend networking events, receptions, and after-hours gatherings to connect with industry peers, potential clients, and thought leaders. Be approachable, listen actively, and exchange contact information for follow-up.

- Engage on Social Media: Use event hashtags and social media platforms to share real-time updates, insights from sessions, and highlights of your booth activities. Monitor social channels for mentions of your company and engage with attendees online.

- Share Content and Resources: Share relevant content such as presentation slides, whitepapers, or recorded demos with prospects who expressed interest.

Provide additional resources that address their specific needs or challenges discussed onsite.

Maximizing your time at industry events requires careful planning, proactive engagement, and strategic follow-up to achieve your business objectives. By leveraging pre-event preparation, optimizing booth presence, engaging in meaningful networking, and executing post-event follow-up, your business can establish a strong presence, build valuable relationships, and drive tangible results that contribute to long-term growth and success in your industry.

Best Practices for Supporting an Industry Event: Enhancing Visibility and Engagement

Industry events present valuable opportunities for businesses to showcase their expertise, connect with stakeholders, and elevate their brand presence within their respective markets. Whether you're sponsoring, exhibiting, or participating in an industry event, strategic support can maximize your impact and achieve meaningful outcomes. Here are best practices to effectively support an industry event and achieve your business objectives:

Define Clear Objectives and Strategy

Before committing to support an industry event, clarify your objectives and align them with your overall business strategy. Whether your goals include lead generation, brand awareness, thought leadership, or networking, having a clear purpose will guide your participation and help measure success.

Choose the Right Events

Select industry events that align with your target audience and business goals. Consider factors such as attendee demographics, industry relevance, geographical location, and event format (e.g., trade shows, conferences, seminars). Prioritize events where your presence will resonate most with potential customers, partners, or industry influencers.

Strategize Your Sponsorship or Exhibition

If sponsoring or exhibiting, leverage your investment by strategically planning your booth design, branding, and promotional materials. Ensure your booth is visually appealing, informative, and aligned with your brand identity. Engage attendees with interactive demonstrations, product showcases, or exclusive offers to attract foot traffic and capture leads.

Maximize Pre-Event Promotion

Utilize pre-event promotion to generate buzz and drive traffic to your booth or session. Leverage event organizers' marketing channels and your own digital platforms (website, social media, email newsletters) to announce your participation, highlight speaking engagements or special activities and invite attendees to visit your booth or attend your session.

Enhance Onsite Engagement

During the event, focus on creating memorable experiences that engage attendees and showcase your value proposition. Train your staff to be knowledgeable, approachable, and proactive in initiating conversations with visitors. Offer personalized demos, host interactive activities or contests, and provide informative materials that resonate with attendees' interests and pain points.

Network and Build Relationships

Take advantage of networking opportunities to connect with industry peers, potential clients, and thought leaders. Attend networking sessions, social events, and after-hours gatherings to foster relationships beyond transactional interactions. Listen actively, exchange insights, and follow up with meaningful connections made during the event.

Measure and Analyze Results

Post-event, evaluate your performance against predefined objectives and KPIs. Measure metrics such as booth traffic, lead quality, engagement levels, and ROI on sponsorship investment. Gather feedback from attendees, assess the success of promotional efforts, and identify areas for improvement in future event strategies.

Follow-Up and Nurture Leads

Promptly follow up with leads and contacts collected during the event. Send personalized thank-you notes, share relevant content or resources, and continue the conversation to nurture relationships. Demonstrate your commitment to meeting their needs and solving the challenges identified during initial interactions.

Share Insights and Thought Leadership

After the event, leverage your participation to establish thought leadership within your industry. Share key takeaways, insights, and trends observed at the event through blog posts, social media updates, or industry publications. Position your company as a knowledgeable resource and engage with a broader audience interested in event topics.

Plan for Continuous Improvement

Use post-event learnings to refine your approach and optimize future event strategies. Document successes, challenges, and actionable insights gathered from attendee interactions and internal debriefs. Incorporate feedback into your event playbook to enhance effectiveness and ensure ongoing alignment with business goals.

Supporting an industry event requires proactive planning, strategic execution, and a commitment to delivering value to attendees, sponsors, and stakeholders. By leveraging best practices before, during, and after the event, businesses can amplify their visibility, strengthen relationships, and achieve meaningful outcomes that contribute to long-term success within their industry.

CHAPTER 18
Understanding Webinars and Podcasts

In today's world, webinars have emerged as a versatile and impactful tool for businesses to engage audiences, share knowledge, and drive growth. Whether you're a startup, SME, or large corporation, harnessing the potential of webinars can significantly enhance your marketing efforts and strengthen your brand presence. Let's explore what webinars are, their benefits, and why they are important for businesses:

A webinar, short for web-based seminar, is a live or pre-recorded presentation, workshop, or seminar conducted over the Internet. Hosted using webinar software platforms, these virtual events enable presenters to deliver content, interact with participants in real-time through features like chat and Q&A, and share multimedia resources such as slides, videos, and polls.

Webinars allow businesses to reach a global audience without the limitations of geographical boundaries. This expanded reach enables:

- **Access to a Wider Audience:** Connect with prospects, clients, and industry stakeholders from different locations, increasing brand visibility and market penetration.

- **Enhanced Engagement:** Facilitate interactive sessions where participants can ask questions, share insights, and engage with speakers and fellow attendees in real-time.

Thought Leadership and Expertise Showcase

Hosting webinars positions businesses as thought leaders within their industry. By:

- Sharing Industry Insights: Provide valuable knowledge, industry trends, and best practices that showcase your expertise and innovation.

- Demonstrating Solutions: Showcase product demonstrations, case studies, and success stories that illustrate your capabilities and address audience pain points effectively.

Lead Generation and Sales Conversion

Webinars are effective lead-generation tools that drive:

- Qualified Leads: Attract prospects interested in your offerings by addressing their specific challenges or interests.

- Sales Opportunities: Nurture leads through informative content, product demos, and exclusive offers presented during webinars, accelerating the sales cycle.

Cost-Effective Marketing Channel

Compared to traditional seminars or workshops, webinars are cost-effective marketing channels that:

- Reduce Overhead Costs: Eliminate travel expenses, venue rentals, and logistical arrangements associated with physical events.

- Scale Efforts: Host multiple sessions or series of webinars to cater to different audience segments or topics without incurring additional expenses.

Data-Driven Insights and Feedback

Webinar platforms provide valuable data and analytics that help businesses:

- Measure Success: Track attendee engagement, webinar attendance rates, and participant feedback to gauge the effectiveness of content and presentation.

- Refine Strategies: Use insights to refine future webinar topics, formats, and promotional strategies based on audience preferences and performance metrics.

Webinars are powerful tools that empower businesses to engage, educate, and convert audiences effectively in today's digital landscape. By leveraging webinars to expand reach, demonstrate thought leadership, generate leads, and gather actionable insights, businesses can drive growth, foster customer relationships, and maintain a competitive edge in their respective markets.

By following these best practices, businesses can effectively manage webinars to engage audiences, demonstrate expertise, and achieve their marketing and business goals. Adjust strategies based on audience feedback and evolving trends to enhance webinar effectiveness and maximize impact continually.

Best Practices for Running a Successful Webinar

Webinars have become a cornerstone of modern business communication, offering a powerful platform to engage audiences, share knowledge, and drive meaningful interactions. Whether you're new to hosting webinars or looking to enhance your webinar strategy, following these best practices can help ensure a seamless and impactful session:

Pre-Webinar Preparation

Define Clear Objectives: Start by setting specific goals for your webinar, whether it's lead generation, brand awareness, or thought leadership.

Choose a Compelling Topic: Select a relevant and engaging topic that addresses your audience's pain points or interests. Tailor your content to provide valuable insights or solutions.

Promote Early and Effectively: Begin promoting your webinar at least 2-3 weeks in advance through email campaigns, social media posts, and on your website. Use compelling visuals and clear messaging to attract registrations.

Tech Check and Rehearsal: Conduct a thorough technical check before the webinar to ensure all equipment, software, and internet connections are stable. Schedule a rehearsal with your speakers to practice transitions and familiarize them with the webinar platform.

During the Webinar

Start Strong: Begin on time with a brief introduction and agenda overview to set expectations. Welcome participants warmly and introduce the speaker(s).

Engage Participants: Encourage interaction throughout the webinar using features like polls, Q&A sessions, and chat. Address questions and comments promptly to keep participants engaged and involved.

Keep to Schedule: Respect your attendees' time by sticking to the planned agenda and timing. Manage transitions between topics smoothly to maintain momentum.

Use Visual Aids Effectively: Enhance your presentation with visually appealing slides, graphics, videos, or live demos. Visual aids help illustrate key points and maintain audience interest.

Post-Webinar Follow-Up

Send Thank-You Emails: Immediately after the webinar, send personalized thank-you emails to attendees. Include a link to the webinar recording, presentation slides, and any additional resources discussed.

Follow-Up with Non-Attendees: Reach out to registered participants who couldn't attend the live session. Provide them with access to the webinar recording and offer to answer any questions they may have.

Collect Feedback: Gather feedback from attendees through surveys or feedback forms. Use this input to evaluate the webinar's effectiveness and identify areas for improvement.

Lead Nurturing: Use attendee data to nurture leads effectively. Provide further content or opportunities that align with their interests and needs based on their webinar engagement.

Running a successful webinar involves careful planning, engaging delivery, and thoughtful follow-up. By following these best practices, businesses can create valuable, interactive experiences that educate, inspire, and foster meaningful connections with their audience. Continuously refine your webinar strategy based on feedback and analytics to maximize engagement and achieve your business objectives effectively.

Embracing webinars as integral components of their marketing and communication strategies enables businesses to adapt to evolving consumer preferences, leverage technology advancements, and capitalize on opportunities for sustained success and market leadership.

Certainly! Here's a blog post on podcasts and their importance to businesses:

Harnessing the Power of Podcasts: A Valuable Asset for Business Growth

In recent years, podcasts have emerged as a dynamic and influential medium in the realm of digital marketing and business communication. With their ability to engage audiences through audio storytelling, interviews, and expert discussions, podcasts offer businesses a unique opportunity to amplify their brand, connect with audiences on a deeper level, and drive meaningful engagement. Let's delve into what podcasts are and why they are increasingly important for businesses today:

What is a Podcast

A podcast is an audio program, typically episodic, that listeners can subscribe to and download or stream online. Podcasts cover a wide range of topics, from industry trends and business strategies to entertainment, personal development, and more. They are accessible via podcast directories like Apple Podcasts, Spotify, Google Podcasts, and podcast apps, allowing listeners to consume content on-demand at their convenience.

Builds Authority and Thought Leadership

Podcasts provide businesses with a platform to showcase their expertise and thought leadership within their industry. By:

- **Sharing Insights:** Discuss industry trends, innovations, and best practices to position your brand as a knowledgeable authority.

- **Interviewing Experts:** Invite industry leaders, influencers, or customers to share their perspectives, enhancing credibility and trust.

Enhances Brand Visibility and Reach

Podcasts enable businesses to reach a broader audience and increase brand awareness through:

- **Content Distribution:** Distribute valuable content to listeners worldwide, expanding your reach beyond traditional marketing channels.

- **Audience Engagement:** Foster a loyal community of listeners who tune in regularly for valuable insights and updates from your brand.

Drives Engagement and Connection

Podcasts offer a personalized and intimate way to engage with your audience:

- **Personal Connection:** Connect with listeners on a personal level through storytelling, anecdotes, and authentic conversations.

- **Interactive Content:** Encourage audience interaction through Q&A segments, listener feedback, and calls-to-action, fostering a sense of community and engagement.

Supports Content Marketing and Lead Generation

Podcasts complement content marketing strategies by:

- **Repurposing Content:** Repurposing podcast episodes into blog posts, social media snippets, or eBooks to extend content longevity and reach.

- **Lead Nurturing:** Use podcasts to nurture leads by providing valuable insights and establishing ongoing communication with potential customers.

Flexibility and Convenience

Podcasts offer flexibility in consumption and production:

- **On-Demand Access:** Listeners can access podcasts anytime, anywhere, making it convenient for busy professionals to stay informed.

- **Ease of Production:** Compared to video content, podcasts require minimal equipment and editing, making them cost-effective and scalable for businesses of all sizes.

Podcasts represent a powerful tool for businesses to enhance brand authority, expand reach, foster engagement, and drive meaningful connections with their audience. By leveraging podcasts as part of their digital marketing and communication strategies, businesses can establish a compelling presence in their industry, nurture customer relationships, and differentiate themselves in a competitive marketplace.

Best Practices for Managing a Podcast for Your Business

Running a podcast for your business involves careful planning, consistent execution, and strategic promotion to maximize engagement and achieve your objectives. Here are some best practices to consider:

1. Define Your Podcast Goals

Set Clear Objectives: Define specific goals for your podcast, such as increasing brand awareness, establishing thought leadership, generating leads, or fostering customer relationships.

Audience Persona: Understand your target audience's preferences, interests, and pain points to tailor content that resonates with them.

2. Plan Your Podcast Content

Choose Relevant Topics: Select topics that align with your business expertise and audience interests. Consider industry trends, customer FAQs, or insightful interviews with industry experts.

Content Calendar: Develop a content calendar outlining episode topics, guest interviews (if applicable), and release schedule to maintain consistency and relevance.

3. Prepare for Production

Invest in Quality Equipment: Ensure clear audio quality by using professional microphones, headphones, and recording software to enhance the listener experience.

Script or Outline: Plan episode structure with an engaging introduction, main discussion points, and a compelling call-to-action.

4. Record and Edit Professionally

Practice and Rehearse: Familiarize yourself with the content and format. Conduct practice runs to refine delivery and ensure smooth transitions.

Editing: Edit recordings to remove background noise, pauses, or errors while maintaining a natural flow and pacing.

5. Optimize for Distribution

Choose a Hosting Platform: Select a reliable podcast hosting platform like Libsyn, Podbean, or Buzzsprout to store and distribute episodes across major podcast directories (e.g., Apple Podcasts, Spotify, Google Podcasts).

Create Compelling Titles and Descriptions: Craft attention-grabbing episode titles and concise descriptions that highlight key topics and entice listeners to tune in.

6. Promote and Market Your Podcast

Cross-Promotion: Leverage your existing marketing channels (website, social media, email newsletters) to promote new episodes and encourage subscriptions.

Guest Promotion: Collaborate with guest speakers to cross-promote episodes to their audience, expanding your podcast's reach organically.

7. Engage with Your Audience

Encourage Feedback and Interaction: Invite listeners to share feedback, ask questions, or suggest future episode topics through social media, email, or dedicated podcast platforms.

Respond Promptly: Engage actively with listeners by responding to comments, questions, and reviews to foster a sense of community and loyalty.

8. Analyze and Iterate

Track Performance Metrics: Monitor download statistics, listener demographics, and engagement metrics provided by your podcast hosting platform to assess performance.

Continuous Improvement: Use listener feedback and analytics to refine content strategy, improve episode quality, and optimize promotional efforts for future episodes.

By following these best practices, businesses can effectively leverage podcasts as a powerful tool to build brand authority, engage audiences, and drive meaningful connections that contribute to long-term business growth and success.

Examples of How To Leverage Podcasts For Your Business

Here are three detailed examples of how businesses can effectively use podcasts to promote their brand and engage with their audience:

Thought Leadership and Industry Insights

Business Type: Management Consulting Firm

Objective: Position the firm as a thought leader in organizational development and strategy consulting.

Podcast Strategy:

- **Podcast Title:** "Strategic Insights in Business Management"
- **Content Focus:** Hosts weekly episodes featuring in-depth discussions on industry trends, case studies,

and interviews with senior consultants and industry experts.

- **Audience Engagement:** Encourages listeners to submit questions or topics for discussion, fostering interaction and addressing audience-specific challenges.

- **Promotion:** Shares podcast episodes across LinkedIn, industry forums, and through email newsletters to reach C-suite executives, HR professionals, and aspiring business leaders.

- **Impact:** Builds credibility, attracts potential clients seeking strategic consulting services, and enhances brand recognition as a trusted advisor in the field of business management.

Customer Education and Product Demonstrations

Business Type: Software as a Service (SaaS) Company

Objective: Educate existing and potential customers about the company's software solutions and functionalities.

Podcast Strategy:

- **Podcast Title:** "SaaS Solutions Unlocked"

- **Content Focus:** Releases bi-weekly episodes discussing various features, updates, and use cases of the software.

- **Customer Stories:** Includes customer testimonials and success stories to illustrate real-world applications and benefits.

- **Integration:** Demonstrates integration capabilities with other business tools and platforms through live demos and expert insights.

- **Promotion:** Promotes episodes on the company's website, within the app interface, and through targeted email campaigns to current users and leads.

- **Impact:** Enhances customer retention, increases product adoption rates, and attracts new users seeking comprehensive software solutions tailored to their business needs.

Brand Storytelling and Community Engagement

Business Type: Outdoor Apparel and Equipment Manufacturer

Objective: Connect with outdoor enthusiasts and eco-conscious consumers, aligning brand values with community interests.

Podcast Strategy:

- **Podcast Title:** "Adventures with [Brand Name]: Stories from the Wild"

- **Content Focus:** Shares inspiring stories from brand ambassadors, athletes, and environmental activists who embody the brand's values of adventure and sustainability.

- **Educational Content:** Discusses outdoor skills, environmental conservation efforts, and tips for responsible outdoor recreation.

- **Community Involvement:** Hosts live recordings at outdoor events, inviting listeners to participate in Q&A sessions and hands-on activities.

- **Promotion:** Shares episodes on social media platforms like Instagram and YouTube, leveraging visually compelling content to resonate with outdoor enthusiasts and nature lovers.

- **Impact:** Strengthens brand loyalty, expands reach within the outdoor community, and attracts environmentally conscious consumers seeking durable and sustainable outdoor gear.

Podcasts offer businesses a versatile platform to engage audiences, share expertise, and build meaningful connections that resonate beyond traditional marketing channels. By strategically aligning podcast content with business objectives, industries, and audience preferences, businesses can effectively promote their brand, nurture customer relationships, and drive long-term growth in a competitive market landscape.

Embrace the potential of podcasts to share your brand's story, connect with your audience authentically, and drive business growth through engaging audio content that resonates with listeners worldwide.

CHAPTER 19
Video Adverting to Promote Business

Video advertising refers to the practice of using video content to promote or advertise products, services, or brands to a targeted audience. It involves creating and distributing video ads across various digital platforms and channels, such as social media, websites, streaming services, and video-sharing platforms like YouTube.

The Power of Videos in Digital Marketing

In the realm of digital marketing, where content is king and engagement is paramount, videos have emerged as a powerhouse tool for businesses to effectively communicate with their audiences, drive engagement, and achieve marketing objectives. From enhancing brand visibility to boosting conversion rates, videos offer a compelling medium to captivate viewers and convey messages in a memorable and impactful way. Let's delve into why videos are crucial for digital marketing strategies and how businesses can leverage their potential for success.

Enhancing Audience Engagement

Videos are inherently more engaging than text or static images due to their:

- **Visual Appeal:** Utilizing dynamic visuals, motion graphics, and compelling storytelling to capture viewer attention and convey complex information effectively.

- **Emotional Connection:** Evoking emotions through storytelling, testimonials, and visual narratives that resonate with audiences on a personal level.

- **Interactivity:** Encouraging viewer interaction through comments, likes, shares, and CTAs embedded within the video to drive further engagement.

Expanding Reach and Accessibility

Videos enable businesses to reach a broader audience across various digital platforms:

- **Platform Diversity:** Publishing videos on YouTube, social media channels (Facebook, Instagram, LinkedIn), and company websites to cater to diverse demographics and preferences.

- **Mobile Optimization:** Meeting the needs of mobile users who consume content on smartphones and tablets, ensuring accessibility anytime, anywhere.

Boosting Conversion Rates and Sales

Videos play a pivotal role in influencing purchasing decisions by:

- **Product Demonstrations:** Showcasing product features, benefits, and use cases to educate and persuade potential customers.

- **Customer Testimonials:** Sharing authentic feedback and success stories from satisfied customers to build trust and credibility.

- **Explainer Videos:** Simplifying complex concepts or processes, enhancing understanding, and motivating viewers to take desired actions.

Improving SEO and Online Visibility

Videos contribute to enhanced search engine optimization (SEO) and online visibility by:

- **Increased Dwell Time:** Keeping visitors engaged longer on your website, signaling search engines about content relevance and quality.

- **Backlink Potential:** Encouraging other websites to link to your videos, boosting domain authority and improving search engine rankings.

- **Social Sharing:** Generating social signals (likes, shares, comments) that contribute to broader organic reach and increased engagement metrics.

Strategies for Effective Video Marketing

Educational Content

Create tutorial videos, how-to guides, or industry insights that provide valuable information and establish your brand as an authority in your niche.

Brand Storytelling

Tell compelling stories about your brand's journey, values, and mission to connect with viewers emotionally and foster brand loyalty.

Product and Service Highlights

Produce videos that highlight new products, services, or updates, showcasing their unique features and benefits to attract and convert potential customers.

Customer Testimonials and Case Studies

Share real-life experiences and success stories from satisfied customers, demonstrating how your offerings have addressed their needs and delivered value.

Harnessing the Power of Digital Advertising: Strategies to Promote Your Business

In today's competitive marketplace, digital advertising has become a cornerstone of successful marketing strategies for businesses looking to expand their reach, attract new customers, and drive growth. With the vast array of digital platforms available, from social media to search engines and beyond, businesses can strategically leverage digital advertising to achieve their marketing goals effectively. Let's explore how you can harness the power of digital advertising to promote your business and achieve measurable results.

Understanding Digital Advertising

Digital advertising encompasses various online strategies and channels used to promote products, services, or brands to a targeted audience. Unlike traditional advertising methods, digital advertising offers precise targeting capabilities, real-time analytics, and the flexibility to adjust campaigns based on performance metrics. Here are key strategies to maximize the impact of your digital advertising efforts:

Define Your Goals and Audience

Before launching any digital advertising campaign, it's crucial to define your objectives and identify your target audience clearly. Consider what you aim to achieve—whether it's increasing brand awareness, driving website traffic, generating leads, or boosting sales. Understanding your audience's demographics, interests, and behaviors will help you tailor your messaging and select the most effective advertising platforms.

Choose the Right Advertising Platforms

Digital advertising offers a plethora of platforms to reach your audience effectively:

- **Search Engine Advertising**: Utilize pay-per-click (PPC) ads on search engines like Google Ads to appear in relevant search results based on keywords related to your business.

- **Social Media Advertising**: Leverage platforms such as Facebook Ads, Instagram Ads, LinkedIn Ads, and Twitter Ads to target specific demographics, interests, or behaviors of users.

- **Display Advertising**: Place banner ads on websites and apps that your target audience frequents, using visual elements to attract attention and drive clicks.

- **Video Advertising**: Run video ads on platforms like YouTube or social media to engage users with compelling visuals and messages.

Craft Compelling Ad Content

Create engaging ad content that resonates with your audience and aligns with your brand's voice and values:

- **Clear Messaging**: Communicate your value proposition succinctly and clearly to capture attention and convey the benefits of your products or services.

- **Visual Appeal**: Use high-quality images, videos, or graphics that attract and maintain viewer interest while reinforcing your brand identity.

- **Strong Call-to-Action (CTA)**: Encourage viewers to take action with a compelling CTA that prompts them to visit your website, make a purchase, sign up for a newsletter, or contact your business.

Implement Targeted Campaigns

Segment your audience and create tailored campaigns that resonate with specific demographics or customer segments:

- **Geotargeting**: Target users based on their location to promote local events, offers, or services relevant to their area.

- **Behavioral Targeting**: Reach users based on their online behaviors, such as past purchases, website visits, or interactions with your brand.

- **Retargeting**: Re-engage users who have previously visited your website or interacted with your ads, reminding them of your products or services and encouraging conversions.

Monitor and Optimize Performance

Regularly monitor the performance of your digital advertising campaigns using analytics tools provided by each platform:

- **Key Metrics**: Track metrics such as click-through rates (CTR), conversion rates, cost-per-click (CPC), and return on ad spend (ROAS) to assess campaign effectiveness.

- **A/B Testing**: Experiment with different ad creatives, audiences, or targeting strategies to identify what resonates best with your audience and optimize your campaigns accordingly.

- **Continuous Improvement**: Use insights gained from analytics to make data-driven decisions, refine your targeting, adjust budgets, and improve the overall performance of your digital advertising efforts.

Digital advertising offers businesses a powerful toolkit to reach and engage with their target audience effectively in today's digital-first world. By defining clear goals, selecting the right platforms, crafting compelling ad content, implementing targeted campaigns, and continuously monitoring performance, businesses can maximize the impact of their digital advertising efforts and achieve significant growth and success.

Explainer Video For Your Website and Social Media

Explainer videos are short, engaging videos typically used to explain complex ideas, products, services, or processes simply and compellingly. They have gained popularity for several compelling reasons:

Why Explainer Videos Are Popular:

1. **Clarity and Simplicity**: Explainer videos distill complex concepts into easily understandable messages using visuals, animations, and narration. They simplify information, making it more accessible and digestible for viewers.

2. **Engagement**: These videos are highly engaging due to their dynamic visuals, storytelling, and often entertaining approach. They capture and maintain viewer attention better than text or static visuals.

3. **Memorability**: Visual content is more memorable than text alone. Explainer videos combine audio-visual elements to create a lasting impression, helping viewers retain information and recall it when needed.

4. **Versatility**: They can be used across various platforms and channels, including websites, social media, presentations, and sales pitches. This versatility allows businesses to reach a wide audience and reinforce their message consistently.

5. **Increased Conversions**: Explainer videos are effective at influencing purchasing decisions by showcasing product benefits, addressing customer pain points, and guiding viewers toward taking specific actions, such as signing up for a service or making a purchase.

6. **SEO Benefits**: Including explainer videos on landing pages or websites can improve search engine optimization (SEO). Videos increase dwell time, reduce bounce rates, and encourage visitors to stay longer on your site, signaling search engines about content relevance and quality.

7. **Brand Building**: By conveying a brand's personality, values, and unique selling propositions, explainer videos help build brand awareness and credibility. They establish trust with audiences and differentiate businesses from competitors.

Types of Explainer Videos:

- **Animated Explainer Videos**: Using animation to simplify complex concepts or abstract ideas, often with characters or scenarios to illustrate key points.

- **Live-Action Explainer Videos**: Featuring real people, products, or settings to demonstrate features, benefits, or usage scenarios.

- **Whiteboard or Hand-drawn Videos**: Utilizing a whiteboard or digital equivalent to illustrate ideas or processes in a step-by-step format, enhancing viewer engagement through visual storytelling.

Explainer videos have become a popular and effective tool for businesses to communicate with their audience, simplify complex information, increase engagement, and drive conversions. Their ability to combine visual appeal, storytelling, and educational value makes them invaluable assets in modern marketing strategies. Businesses across various industries continue to leverage explainer videos to enhance brand communication, educate customers, and achieve their marketing objectives effectively in today's digital age.

Best Practices for Building Explainer Videos For Your Business

Creating an effective explainer video involves several best practices to ensure it effectively communicates your message and engages your audience. Here are key practices to consider when creating an explainer video:

Define Your Goal and Audience

- **Clarity on Purpose**: Clearly define the goal of your explainer video—whether it's to introduce a new product, explain a service, educate about a process, or increase brand awareness.

- **Audience Understanding**: Know your target audience's demographics, interests, pain points, and preferences to tailor the video content and messaging appropriately.

Script and Storyboard Development

- **Clear Structure**: Develop a concise script that outlines the key message and flow of the video. Start with a compelling hook to grab attention, followed by the main content, and conclude with a strong call-to-action (CTA).

- **Storyboarding**: Create a visual storyboard that maps out the scenes, transitions, and visual elements of the video. This helps visualize how the narrative will unfold and ensures a cohesive story flow.

Keep it Concise and Engaging

- **Short and Sweet**: Keep the video duration between 60 to 90 seconds for optimal engagement. Capture attention quickly and maintain interest throughout the video to prevent viewer drop-off.

- **Visual Appeal**: Use high-quality visuals, animations, and graphics that align with your brand's aesthetics and appeal to your target audience. Visual storytelling should complement the script and enhance understanding.

Use Professional Voiceover and Music

- **Voiceover Quality**: Hire a professional voiceover artist whose tone, pace, and style resonate with your brand and target audience. Ensure the voiceover is clear, expressive, and aligned with the video's message.

- **Background Music**: Incorporate background music that enhances the mood and reinforces the video's narrative without overpowering the voiceover. Choose royalty-free music to avoid copyright issues.

Focus on Benefits and Solutions

- **Address Pain Points**: Clearly articulate how your product or service solves a problem or addresses a customer's pain point. Highlight benefits and unique selling propositions (USPs) to demonstrate value to the viewer.

- **Visual Demonstrations**: Use animations or screen recordings to demonstrate product features, user interface (UI), or process steps effectively. This helps viewers visualize how your offering works in real-world scenarios.

Include a Strong Call-to-Action (CTA)

- **Direct CTA**: End the video with a clear and compelling CTA that prompts viewers to take action, such as visiting your website, signing up for a trial, contacting your sales team, or making a purchase.

Optimize for Distribution and SEO

- **Platform Compatibility**: Ensure the video is optimized for various platforms and devices, including desktops, smartphones, and tablets. Use formats and resolutions that support seamless playback across different channels.

- **SEO Optimization**: Include relevant keywords in the video title, description, and tags to improve discoverability on search engines and video-sharing platforms like YouTube. Link the video to related content on your website for cross-promotion.

Test and Iterate

- **Feedback Loop**: Gather feedback from internal stakeholders or a focus group to refine the video content, messaging, and visual elements. Test different versions or edits to optimize engagement and effectiveness.

- **Performance Tracking**: Monitor key performance indicators (KPIs) such as view count, engagement rate, click-through rate (CTR), and conversion rate. Use analytics to measure the video's impact and make data-driven decisions for future videos.

Creating an effective explainer video requires careful planning, creative execution, and a deep understanding of your audience and objectives. By following these best practices—from defining clear goals and audience to crafting engaging content and optimizing for distribution—you can create compelling explainer videos that effectively communicate your message, engage viewers, and drive desired actions for your business. Incorporate these practices into your video production process to maximize the impact and success of your explainer video campaigns.

Embrace the potential of video marketing as a strategic asset to elevate your digital presence, engage with your audience, and achieve meaningful business outcomes. Start integrating videos into your digital marketing strategy today to stay ahead of the curve and unlock new opportunities for growth.

CHAPTER 20
Developing Digital Marketing Campaigns

Digital Marketing Campaign

A digital marketing campaign is a structured effort to promote a product, service, or brand using online channels and digital tools. Unlike traditional marketing campaigns that rely on print ads, billboards, or TV commercials, digital marketing campaigns leverage the internet and digital platforms such as social media, email, search engines, and websites. The primary goal is to reach a targeted audience, engage them, and drive specific actions such as purchasing a product, signing up for a newsletter, or downloading a whitepaper. Digital marketing campaigns are highly versatile, allowing businesses to tailor their strategies to their unique needs and goals.

Goal Setting and Audience Targeting

The foundation of a successful digital marketing campaign lies in setting clear, measurable goals. These objectives should align with the overall business strategy and can range from increasing brand awareness to driving sales or generating leads. Once the goals are established, the next crucial step is identifying the target audience. Understanding who the potential customers are, including their demographics, interests, and online behaviors, allows businesses to create personalized content and choose the right platforms to reach them effectively. This targeted approach ensures that the marketing efforts resonate with the intended audience, increasing the likelihood of achieving the campaign's objectives.

Content Creation and Channel Selection

Content is the backbone of any digital marketing campaign. It includes everything from blog posts, social media updates, and emails to videos, infographics, and ads. The content should be engaging, informative, and aligned with the campaign's goals and the audience's preferences. Additionally, selecting the right channels to distribute the content is crucial. Different platforms serve different purposes and attract various audiences. For example, LinkedIn is ideal for B2B marketing, while Instagram and Facebook are more suited for B2C campaigns. By strategically choosing where to publish content, businesses can maximize their reach and engagement.

Execution and Monitoring

Executing a digital marketing campaign involves rolling out the planned content across the selected channels and actively engaging with the audience. This phase requires diligent monitoring to track the campaign's performance and make necessary adjustments. Tools like Google Analytics, social media insights, and email marketing software provide valuable data on metrics such as website traffic, click-through rates, conversion rates, and social media engagement. Regular monitoring helps identify what is working and what isn't, allowing marketers to optimize their strategies in real-time and ensure the campaign remains on track to meet its goals.

Measuring Success and Optimization

The final stage of a digital marketing campaign is measuring its success against predefined goals and optimizing future efforts. This involves analyzing the collected data to assess the campaign's overall impact and ROI. Key performance indicators (KPIs) like increased sales, higher engagement rates, or improved brand recognition provide insights into the campaign's effectiveness. Based on these insights, businesses can refine their future campaigns, making them more targeted and efficient. Continuous learning and adaptation are essential in digital marketing, ensuring that each campaign builds on the success and lessons of the previous ones, driving sustained growth and improvement over time.

The Benefits of Digital Marketing Campaigns for a Business

Increased Reach and Visibility

Digital marketing campaigns allow businesses to reach a wider audience than traditional marketing methods. Through the use of online platforms such as social media, search engines, and email marketing, businesses can connect with potential customers worldwide. This increased reach helps businesses tap into new markets and expand their customer base beyond geographical limitations.

Example: A small local bakery can use social media marketing to attract customers not just from its immediate vicinity but from neighboring towns and cities. By posting appealing photos of their products and engaging with customers online, they can significantly boost their visibility and attract more foot traffic to their store.

Cost-Effectiveness

Digital marketing is often more cost-effective than traditional marketing. Online advertising platforms like Google Ads and social media ads allow businesses to set their own budgets and target specific audiences, ensuring that marketing dollars are spent efficiently. Additionally, digital marketing campaigns provide real-time data and analytics, enabling businesses to measure ROI and adjust strategies promptly.

Example: A startup with a limited marketing budget can use targeted Facebook ads to reach a specific demographic interested in their product. By setting a daily budget and optimizing the ads based on performance metrics, they can achieve a high return on investment without spending excessively on broad, untargeted advertising.

Measurable Results and Analytics

One of the significant advantages of digital marketing campaigns is the ability to measure results accurately. Tools like Google Analytics, social media insights, and email marketing software provide detailed data on campaign performance, including metrics like click-through rates, conversion rates, and customer engagement. This data helps businesses understand what works and what doesn't, enabling them to make data-driven decisions and optimize their campaigns for better results.

Example: An e-commerce store running a digital marketing campaign can track which ads generate the most clicks and conversions, analyze the behavior of visitors on their website, and determine the most effective channels for driving sales. This data-driven approach allows them to refine their strategies and allocate resources to the most impactful marketing activities.

Enhanced Customer Engagement and Interaction

Digital marketing campaigns facilitate direct interaction with customers, fostering stronger relationships and brand loyalty. Through social media platforms, businesses can engage with their audience by responding to comments, addressing concerns, and participating in conversations. This level of engagement builds trust and creates a sense of community around the brand.

Example: A fashion brand can use Instagram to showcase its latest collections, run contests, and share behind-the-scenes content. By actively engaging with followers through comments and direct messages, they can create a loyal customer base that feels connected to the brand and is more likely to make repeat purchases.

Flexibility and Adaptability

Digital marketing campaigns offer flexibility and adaptability, allowing businesses to quickly respond to changing market conditions and customer preferences. Campaigns can be adjusted in real-time based on performance data, and new strategies can be implemented without the long lead times associated with traditional marketing.

Example: A software company launching a new product can start with a targeted email marketing campaign. Based on the initial response, they can quickly tweak the messaging, change the target audience, or introduce additional promotional offers to maximize engagement and conversions. This agility ensures that marketing efforts remain relevant and effective in a dynamic market environment.

Digital marketing campaigns provide numerous benefits for businesses, including increased reach and visibility, cost-effectiveness, measurable results, enhanced customer engagement, and flexibility. By leveraging the power of digital marketing, businesses can connect with their target audience more effectively, optimize their marketing spend, and drive sustainable growth. Whether you're a small business or a large corporation, investing in digital marketing can help you stay competitive and achieve your business goals in today's digital age.

Creating and Managing a Digital Marketing Campaign

Setting Clear Goals

Before diving into the specifics, it's crucial to establish what you want to achieve with your digital marketing campaign. For this example, let's assume you are launching a new eco-friendly product line, and your primary goals are to increase brand awareness and drive online sales.

Goals:

- Increase brand awareness by 50% within three months

- Achieve 1,000 product sales within the first three months

Identifying the Target Audience

Understanding your audience is essential. For this campaign, you're targeting environmentally conscious consumers aged 25-45 who are interested in sustainable products.

Target Audience:

- Age: 25-45

- Interests: Sustainability, eco-friendly products, organic living

- Online Behavior: Active on social media (Instagram, Facebook), frequent online shoppers, follow eco-conscious influencers

Budget Allocation

Determining the budget is a crucial step. For this example, let's allocate $10,000 for the campaign, distributed across various channels and activities.

Budget Breakdown:

- Social Media Advertising (Instagram, Facebook): $4,000

- Content Creation (Videos, Blog Posts, Infographics): $2,000

- Influencer Partnerships: $2,000

- Email Marketing: $1,000

- Analytics and Monitoring Tools: $1,000

Choosing the Right Channels and Creating Content

Selecting the appropriate channels and creating engaging content tailored to your audience is vital.

Channels:

- Social Media: Use Instagram and Facebook for targeted ads and organic posts.

- Email Marketing: Send out newsletters and promotional emails to your existing customer base.

- Influencer Marketing: Partner with eco-conscious influencers to reach a broader audience.

- Content Marketing: Publish blog posts and create videos that highlight the benefits of your eco-friendly product line.

Content Ideas:

- Videos: Short explainer videos about the sustainability of your products.

- Blog Posts: Articles on the importance of eco-friendly living and how your products contribute.

- Social Media Posts: Eye-catching graphics and stories showcasing your products in use.

- Emails: Engaging newsletters with product information, customer testimonials, and special offers.

Executing the Campaign

Roll out the content according to a well-structured plan. Schedule posts, ads, and emails to ensure consistent and timely communication.

Execution Plan:

- Week 1: Launch teaser posts on social media and start influencer collaborations.

- Week 2: Publish a blog post and send out an introductory email.

- Week 3: Release the first video on social media and run targeted ads.

- Week 4: Share customer testimonials and behind-the-scenes content.

- Ongoing: Regularly post updates, engage with the audience, and adjust ads based on performance.

Monitoring and Optimization

Track the campaign's progress using analytics tools. Monitor key metrics such as engagement rates, click-through rates (CTR), conversion rates, and sales.

Tools:

- Google Analytics: Monitor website traffic and user behavior.

- Social Media Insights: Track engagement, reach, and ad performance on Instagram and Facebook.

- Email Marketing Software: Measure open rates, click-through rates, and conversions from email campaigns.

Measuring Success and Refining Strategies

At the end of the campaign, analyze the data to measure success against your goals. Identify what worked well and what didn't and use these insights to refine future campaigns.

Analysis:

- Brand Awareness: Check if there was a 50% increase in social media followers, website visits, and mentions.

- Sales: Verify if 1,000 product sales were achieved within the timeframe.

Optimization:

- Content: Determine which types of content (videos, blog posts, social media posts) had the highest engagement and conversions.

- Channels: Assess which platforms (Instagram, Facebook, email) were most effective.

- Budget: Reallocate the budget based on the most cost-effective channels and tactics.

By following these steps, you can create and manage a successful digital marketing campaign that effectively promotes your product, engages your audience, and achieves your business goals.

RESOURCES NEEDED TO MANAGE DIGITAL MARKETING CAMPAIGN

Managing a successful digital marketing campaign requires a combination of tools, skills, and resources. Here's a comprehensive look at the essential resources needed:

Personnel and Expertise

- Digital Marketing Strategist: Develops and oversees the overall campaign strategy, ensuring alignment with business goals.

- Content Creators: Writers, designers, and videographers who create engaging content such as blog posts, social media updates, videos, infographics, and more.

- SEO Specialists: Optimize content for search engines to improve organic search rankings.

- Social Media Managers: Handle social media accounts, engage with the audience, and manage paid social media campaigns.

- Paid Advertising Specialists: Manage PPC campaigns on platforms like Google Ads, Facebook Ads, and other paid advertising channels.

- Email Marketing Experts: Develop and manage email marketing campaigns, segment lists, and analyze email performance.

- Web Developers: Ensure the website is optimized, user-friendly, and integrated with analytics tools.

- Analytics Experts: Analyze campaign data and metrics to measure performance and provide insights for optimization.

Tools and Software

- Content Management System (CMS): Platforms like WordPress or HubSpot for creating and managing website content.

- Social Media Management Tools: Tools like Hootsuite, Buffer, or Sprout Social for scheduling posts, managing multiple accounts, and analyzing social media performance.

- SEO Tools: Platforms like SEMrush, Ahrefs, or Moz for keyword research, backlink analysis, and site audits.

- Email Marketing Software: Tools like Mailchimp, Constant Contact, or SendinBlue for creating and managing email campaigns.

- Analytics and Reporting Tools: Google Analytics, Google Data Studio, and other reporting tools to track website traffic, user behavior, and campaign performance.

- Ad Management Platforms: Google Ads, Facebook Ads Manager, LinkedIn Ads, and other platforms for managing PPC campaigns.

- Graphic Design and Video Editing Tools: Adobe Creative Cloud, Canva, and video editing software like Final Cut Pro or Adobe Premiere Pro for creating visual content.

- Customer Relationship Management (CRM) Systems: Tools like Salesforce, HubSpot, or Zoho CRM for managing customer interactions and data.

Budget

- Advertising Spend: Allocate the budget for paid advertising on search engines, social media platforms, and other digital channels.

- Content Creation: Budget for hiring content creators, designers, videographers, and other professionals as needed.

- Tool Subscriptions: Budget for subscribing to the necessary digital marketing tools and software.

- Training and Development: Invest in ongoing training and development for the digital marketing team to stay updated with the latest trends and technologies.

Content and Creative Assets

- Blog Posts and Articles: Well-researched and optimized content for attracting and engaging the audience.

- Social Media Content: Engaging posts, stories, and videos tailored to different social media platforms.

- Email Campaigns: Newsletters, promotional emails, and automated email sequences.

- Ad Creatives: Banners, images, videos, and ad copy for paid campaigns.

- Landing Pages: Optimized landing pages for lead generation and conversion.

Data and Insights

- Audience Data: Information about the target audience's demographics, interests, and online behavior.

- Competitor Analysis: Insights into competitor strategies and performance to identify opportunities and threats.

- Market Trends: Current trends and developments in the industry to keep the campaign relevant and effective.

Planning and Coordination

- Campaign Calendar: A detailed timeline outlining key milestones, content publishing dates, and campaign phases.

- Project Management Tools: Tools like Asana, Trello, or Monday.com to manage tasks, collaborate with team members, and track progress.

- Communication Tools: Platforms like Slack, Microsoft Teams, or Zoom for effective communication and collaboration among team members.

Example of Digital Marketing Campaign: E-commerce Business Launching a New Product Line

Objective: Increase brand awareness and drive sales for a new eco-friendly product line.

1. **Strategy Development:**

   o Digital Marketing Strategist outlines the campaign goals, target audience, and key messages.

2. **Content Creation:**

   o Content Creators develop blog posts, social media content, email newsletters, and videos showcasing the new products.

3. **SEO and Website Optimization:**

   o SEO Specialists optimize product pages and blog posts for relevant keywords.

   o Web Developers ensure the website is user-friendly and fast-loading.

4. **Social Media and Advertising:**

   o Social Media Managers schedule regular posts and engage with followers.

   o Paid Advertising Specialists create and manage PPC campaigns on Google Ads and social media platforms.

5. **Email Marketing:**

   o Email Marketing Experts create a series of automated emails to announce the product launch and offer exclusive discounts.

6. **Analytics and Reporting:**

   o Analytics Experts monitor campaign performance using Google Analytics and other tools, providing regular reports and insights for optimization.

7. **Budget Management:**

   o Allocate the budget for content creation, advertising spending, tool subscriptions, and other necessary expenses.

A PRACTICAL GUIDE TO DIGITAL MARKETING

By leveraging the right combination of personnel, tools, content, and data, businesses can create and manage effective digital marketing campaigns that drive growth and achieve their marketing objectives.

BEST PRACTICES FOR CREATING AND MANAGING A DIGITAL MARKETING CAMPAIGN

Creating and executing a successful digital marketing campaign involves a blend of strategic planning, creative execution, and continuous optimization. Here are the best practices to guide you through the process:

Set Clear and Measurable Goals

Best Practice: Establish Specific, Measurable, Achievable, Relevant, and Time-bound (SMART) goals.

Example: Instead of aiming to "increase website traffic," set a goal to "increase website traffic by 25% over the next three months through targeted content marketing and social media advertising."

Understand Your Target Audience

Best Practice: Develop detailed buyer personas to understand your audience's needs, behaviors, and preferences.

Example: Create personas based on demographic data, purchasing habits, online behavior, and pain points to tailor your marketing messages effectively.

Conduct Competitor Analysis

Best Practice: Analyze your competitors to identify their strengths, weaknesses, and marketing strategies.

Example: Use tools like SEMrush, Ahrefs, or SimilarWeb to study competitors' keywords, backlinks, and traffic sources and identify gaps in your own strategy.

Choose the Right Channels

Best Practice: Select digital marketing channels that align with your audience and goals.

Example: If your audience is highly active on social media, focus on platforms like Instagram, Facebook, and LinkedIn. If they prefer consuming long-form content, invest in blogging and SEO.

Develop a Content Strategy

Best Practice: Create valuable, relevant, and consistent content to attract and engage your audience.

Example: Plan a mix of blog posts, videos, infographics, and social media updates that address your audience's pain points and provide solutions.

Optimize for SEO

Best Practice: Ensure your website and content are optimized for search engines to improve organic visibility.

Example: Conduct keyword research using tools like Google Keyword Planner or Moz, and incorporate relevant keywords into your content, meta tags, and URLs.

Leverage Social Media

Best Practice: Use social media platforms to build relationships with your audience, share content, and run targeted ads.

Example: Schedule regular posts, engage with followers, and use social media ads to reach a broader audience with specific targeting options.

Implement Email Marketing

Best Practice: Build and segment your email list to send personalized and relevant messages.

Example: Use email marketing tools like Mailchimp or Constant Contact to create automated email sequences that nurture leads and drive conversions.

Invest in Paid Advertising

Best Practice: Use PPC campaigns to drive targeted traffic and achieve quick results.

Example: Run Google Ads for high-intent keywords and Facebook Ads for demographic targeting, continuously optimizing based on performance data.

Track and Analyze Performance

Best Practice: Use analytics tools to measure the performance of your campaigns and gain insights.

Example: Utilize Google Analytics, social media insights, and email marketing reports to track key metrics such as traffic, engagement, conversions, and ROI.

A/B Testing

Best Practice: Conduct A/B tests to compare different versions of your content, ads, or landing pages and determine what works best.

Example: Test different headlines, images, or calls-to-action (CTAs) in your ads to see which combination yields the highest conversion rates.

Continuous Optimization

Best Practice: Regularly review your campaign performance and make data-driven adjustments to improve results.

Example: If certain keywords or ad creatives perform better, allocate more budget to those areas and refine underperforming elements.

Example of a Digital Marketing Campaign Execution Plan

Pre-Campaign Planning

1. Goal Setting: Define SMART goals for the campaign.

2. Audience Research: Develop buyer personas and understand audience behavior.

3. Competitor Analysis: Identify competitors' strategies and performance.

4. Channel Selection: Choose the most effective channels for your audience.

5. Content Planning: Create a content calendar with planned posts, articles, videos, etc.

Campaign Execution

1. Content Creation: Develop high-quality content tailored to your audience.

2. SEO Optimization: Optimize all content and website pages for search engines.

3. Social Media Engagement: Post regularly, engage with followers and run targeted ads.

4. Email Marketing: Send out newsletters and promotional emails to segmented lists.

5. Paid Advertising: Launch PPC campaigns on Google Ads, Facebook Ads, etc.

Post-Campaign Analysis

1. Performance Tracking: Use analytics tools to measure key metrics.

2. A/B Testing: Test different elements of your campaign to optimize performance.

3. Optimization: Adjust strategies based on data insights to improve future campaigns.

4. Reporting: Compile and review campaign performance reports to assess success and areas for improvement.

Creating and executing a successful digital marketing campaign involves thorough planning, continuous monitoring, and strategic adjustments. By setting clear goals, understanding your audience, leveraging the right channels, and continuously optimizing based on data, you can maximize the effectiveness of your digital marketing efforts and achieve your business objectives.

CHAPTER 21
Understanding Marketing Data and Analytics

Understanding Marketing Data and Analytics

Marketing data and analytics encompass the collection, measurement, analysis, and interpretation of data related to marketing activities. This process enables businesses to understand the effectiveness of their marketing strategies, make data-driven decisions, and optimize future campaigns for better results. With the vast amount of data generated from various digital marketing channels, it has become crucial for businesses to leverage analytics to stay competitive and meet the evolving needs of their customers.

The Role of Data in Marketing

Data plays a pivotal role in modern marketing by providing insights into consumer behavior, preferences, and trends. By collecting data from multiple touchpoints such as websites, social media, email campaigns, and advertisements, marketers can gain a comprehensive view of their audience. This information helps in creating targeted marketing campaigns that resonate with specific segments of the market, ultimately leading to higher engagement and conversion rates. Data-driven marketing enables businesses to move away from a one-size-fits-all approach and adopt personalized strategies that cater to individual customer needs.

Types of Marketing Data

Marketing data can be categorized into several types, each serving a unique purpose. Descriptive data provides an overview of what has happened in past marketing activities, such as website visits, click-through rates, and sales figures. Diagnostic data helps in understanding the reasons behind certain outcomes, such as why a particular campaign performed better than others. Predictive data uses historical information and advanced algorithms to forecast future trends and behaviors, allowing marketers to anticipate customer needs. Prescriptive data, on the other hand, offers actionable recommendations to optimize marketing strategies based on predictive insights.

Tools and Technologies for Data Collection

A plethora of tools and technologies are available for collecting and analyzing marketing data. Google Analytics, for instance, is a widely used platform that provides detailed insights into website traffic, user behavior, and conversion rates. Social media analytics tools like Hootsuite and Sprout Social offer metrics on engagement, reach, and audience demographics. Email marketing platforms such as Mailchimp and Constant Contact track open rates, click-through rates, and subscriber behavior. Additionally, Customer Relationship Management (CRM) systems like Salesforce and HubSpot integrate data from various sources to give a holistic view of customer interactions.

Analyzing Marketing Data

Analyzing marketing data involves transforming raw data into meaningful insights. This process includes cleaning the data to remove inaccuracies, organizing it into a structured format, and applying statistical methods to uncover patterns and trends. Visualization tools like Tableau and Power BI are commonly used to create interactive dashboards and reports that present data in an easily understandable format. Through data analysis, marketers can identify which campaigns are driving the most traffic, which channels are most effective, and where improvements can be made.

The Impact of Analytics on Decision-Making

Marketing analytics significantly enhances decision-making by providing a factual basis for strategy development. Instead of relying on intuition or guesswork, marketers can use data-driven insights to determine the best course of action. For example, if analytics reveal that a particular demographic is highly responsive to email campaigns, a business can allocate more resources to that channel. Moreover, real-time analytics allow marketers to make timely adjustments to ongoing campaigns, ensuring optimal performance and return on investment.

Challenges in Marketing Data and Analytics

Despite its numerous benefits, marketing data and analytics come with challenges. One of the primary issues is data integration, as businesses often use multiple platforms that do not communicate with each other seamlessly. Ensuring data accuracy and consistency across these platforms can be daunting. Additionally, interpreting data requires a certain level of expertise, and not all businesses have access to skilled data analysts. Privacy concerns and regulatory compliance also pose significant challenges, as businesses must handle customer data responsibly and adhere to laws such as GDPR and CCPA.

The Future of Marketing Analytics

The future of marketing analytics lies in advancements in artificial intelligence (AI) and machine learning (ML). These technologies are capable of processing vast amounts of data quickly and uncovering insights that humans might miss.

Predictive analytics, powered by AI, can offer more accurate forecasts and personalized recommendations. As technology continues to evolve, marketing analytics will become even more sophisticated, enabling businesses to understand their customers better and create highly targeted marketing strategies. Embracing these innovations will be crucial for businesses aiming to stay ahead in a competitive landscape.

Benefits of Marketing Data and Analytics for Business

Marketing data and analytics provide numerous benefits to businesses by offering deep insights into customer behavior, optimizing marketing strategies, and enhancing decision-making processes. Here are some key benefits with examples:

Improved Customer Understanding

Benefit: Marketing data and analytics allow businesses to gain a comprehensive understanding of their customers' preferences, behaviors, and demographics.

Example: A retail company can analyze purchase histories, website interactions, and social media engagement to identify the most popular products and preferred shopping times. This information helps in creating personalized marketing messages and offers, increasing customer satisfaction and loyalty.

Enhanced Targeting and Personalization

Benefit: Data-driven insights enable businesses to segment their audience more effectively and deliver personalized content and offers.

Example: An e-commerce business can use analytics to segment its customer base into different groups based on purchase behavior, geographic location, and browsing history. By tailoring email campaigns to these specific segments, the business can increase open rates, click-through rates, and, ultimately, sales conversions.

Optimized Marketing Spend

Benefit: Marketing data helps businesses allocate their budget more efficiently by identifying the most effective channels and campaigns.

Example: A company running multiple digital ad campaigns can use analytics to track the performance of each campaign across various platforms. By analyzing metrics such as cost-per-click (CPC), conversion rates, and return on ad spend (ROAS), the company can identify which campaigns yield the highest returns and allocate more budget to those while reducing spend on underperforming ones.

Enhanced Customer Experience

Benefit: Understanding customer interactions and feedback allows businesses to improve their overall customer experience.

Example: A service-based business can use data from customer feedback surveys, social media comments, and support tickets to identify common pain points and areas for improvement. By addressing these issues proactively, the business can enhance customer satisfaction and retention.

Real-Time Insights and Agility

Benefit: Real-time data analytics provide businesses with up-to-date information, allowing them to react quickly to changing market conditions and customer behaviors.

Example: An online retailer can monitor website traffic and sales in real-time during a major promotional event. If analytics indicate that a particular product is selling out faster than expected, the retailer can quickly adjust inventory levels, update marketing messages, and reallocate resources to maximize sales opportunities.

Predictive Analytics and Forecasting

Benefit: Predictive analytics use historical data to forecast future trends, helping businesses make informed strategic decisions.

Example: A subscription-based service can use predictive analytics to forecast customer churn rates. By identifying factors that contribute to customer attrition, the business can implement targeted retention strategies, such as personalized offers or improved customer support, to reduce churn and increase customer lifetime value.

Improved Campaign Effectiveness

Benefit: Data analytics provide insights into the performance of marketing campaigns, enabling continuous optimization for better results.

Example: A B2B company running a content marketing campaign can use analytics to measure metrics such as website traffic, lead generation, and content engagement. By identifying which types of content resonate most with its audience, the company can refine its content strategy to produce more high-performing content, thereby increasing lead generation and conversion rates.

Competitive Advantage

Benefit: Leveraging marketing data and analytics can give businesses a competitive edge by uncovering insights that competitors may overlook.

Example: A company can analyze competitor performance using tools like SEMrush or Ahrefs to identify gaps in their SEO strategy. By understanding which keywords competitors are ranking for and where they are lacking, the company can adjust its own SEO efforts to capture more organic search traffic and outperform competitors in search engine rankings.

Data-Driven Product Development

Benefit: Marketing analytics can inform product development by identifying customer needs and market trends.

Example: A technology company can analyze customer feedback, usage data, and market trends to identify features that users want in their software products. By prioritizing these features in their development roadmap, the company can create products that better meet customer expectations and drive higher adoption rates.

Measurement and Accountability

Benefit: Marketing data and analytics provide measurable results, allowing businesses to hold their marketing efforts accountable and demonstrate ROI.

Example: A financial services firm can track the performance of its digital marketing campaigns through detailed analytics reports. By measuring metrics such as lead generation, conversion rates, and customer acquisition costs, the firm can quantify the return on investment for each campaign and make data-driven decisions to optimize future marketing efforts.

In summary, marketing data and analytics are essential tools for businesses looking to improve customer understanding, enhance targeting and personalization, optimize marketing spend, and gain a competitive advantage. By leveraging data-driven insights, businesses can make informed decisions, deliver better customer experiences, and achieve their marketing objectives more effectively.

Best Practices: Leveraging Marketing Data and Analytics to Grow a Business

Leveraging marketing data and analytics effectively can significantly contribute to the growth of a business. Here are some best practices, along with examples, to illustrate how businesses can harness the power of data to drive growth:

Set Clear Objectives

Best Practice: Define specific, measurable, achievable, relevant, and time-bound (SMART) goals for your marketing efforts.

Example: Instead of setting a vague goal like "increase website traffic," set a SMART goal such as "increase website traffic by 20% over the next three months through content marketing and social media advertising."

Centralize Data Collection

Best Practice: Use integrated tools and platforms to centralize data collection from various marketing channels.

Example: Utilize a Customer Relationship Management (CRM) system like Salesforce to gather data from email campaigns, social media interactions, website visits, and sales transactions. This centralized approach provides a holistic view of customer interactions and marketing performance.

Analyze Customer Behavior

Best Practice: Use analytics to understand customer behavior and preferences.

Example: An e-commerce business can analyze browsing patterns, purchase history, and cart abandonment rates to identify common reasons why customers abandon their carts. By addressing these issues, such as by offering personalized discounts or improving the checkout process, the business can increase conversion rates.

Segment Your Audience

Best Practice: Segment your audience based on demographics, behavior, and preferences to deliver personalized marketing messages.

Example: A fashion retailer can segment its audience into groups such as "frequent buyers," "seasonal shoppers," and "new customers." Tailored email campaigns can then be created for each segment, offering relevant products and promotions. Frequent buyers might receive loyalty rewards, while new customers might get welcome discounts.

Implement Predictive Analytics

Best Practice: Use predictive analytics to forecast future trends and customer behaviors.

Example: A subscription-based service can use predictive analytics to identify customers who are likely to churn. By analyzing past behavior and engagement levels, the service can proactively reach out to these customers with personalized retention offers, reducing churn rates and increasing customer lifetime value.

Optimize Marketing Campaigns

Best Practice: Continuously monitor and optimize marketing campaigns based on data insights.

Example: A digital marketing agency running PPC campaigns can use A/B testing to compare different ad creatives, landing pages, and bidding strategies. By analyzing which variations perform best, the agency can optimize the campaigns to achieve higher click-through rates and lower cost-per-acquisition.

Leverage Social Media Insights

Best Practice: Utilize social media analytics to understand audience engagement and preferences.

Example: A beauty brand can use social media analytics tools like Hootsuite or Sprout Social to track engagement metrics, such as likes, shares, and comments. By identifying the types of content that resonate most with their audience (e.g., tutorial videos, user-generated content), the brand can focus on creating more of this content to boost engagement and brand loyalty.

Measure ROI and Attribution

Best Practice: Use data to measure the return on investment (ROI) and attribution of different marketing channels.

Example: A B2B company can use marketing analytics tools to track the customer's journey from initial contact to final sale. By understanding which channels (e.g., email, social media, paid search) contribute most to conversions, the company can allocate its marketing budget more effectively to maximize ROI.

Create Data-Driven Content

Best Practice: Develop content based on data insights to address customer needs and interests.

Example: A health and wellness blog can use keyword research and Google Analytics to identify popular search terms and topics. By creating high-quality content around these topics, the blog can attract more organic traffic and establish itself as an authority in the niche.

Foster a Data-Driven Culture

Best Practice: Encourage a data-driven culture within your organization by providing training and resources for data literacy.

Example: A marketing team can attend workshops and use online courses to improve their skills in data analysis and interpretation. By fostering a culture where decisions are based on data rather than intuition, the team can develop more effective and strategic marketing campaigns.

Use Visualization Tools

Best Practice: Utilize data visualization tools to present data in an easily understandable format.

Example: A retail chain can use Tableau or Power BI to create interactive dashboards that display key performance indicators (KPIs) such as sales trends, inventory levels, and customer demographics. These visualizations help stakeholders quickly grasp insights and make informed decisions.

Conduct Regular Data Audits

Best Practice: Perform regular audits of your marketing data to ensure accuracy and consistency.

Example: An online marketplace can periodically review its data collection processes and tools to ensure that the data being gathered is accurate and up-to-date. This includes checking for duplicate entries, outdated information, and inconsistencies across different data sources.

EXAMPLES of BRANDS USE of MARKETING DATA for BUSINESS

Brands across various industries are leveraging marketing data to improve their strategies, enhance customer experiences, and drive business growth. Here are three detailed examples:

Netflix: Personalization and Content Recommendations

How They're Using Marketing Data: Netflix uses marketing data to personalize user experiences and recommend content based on viewing habits, preferences, and behaviors. The streaming giant collects data on what users watch, how long they watch, when they pause or stop, and their ratings for shows and movies.

Benefits:

- Enhanced User Experience: By analyzing viewing patterns and preferences, Netflix can recommend shows and movies that are more likely to interest individual users, keeping them engaged on the platform longer.

- Increased Retention Rates: Personalized recommendations help retain subscribers by continuously offering content that aligns with their tastes.

- Content Creation: Data insights help Netflix decide which types of shows and movies to produce or acquire, ensuring they invest in content that will likely be popular with their audience.

Starbucks: Loyalty Programs and Customer Engagement

How They're Using Marketing Data: Starbucks uses its mobile app and loyalty program to gather extensive data on customer purchases, preferences, and behaviors. This data includes what products customers buy, at what times, and how often.

Benefits:

- Personalized Promotions: Starbucks uses this data to send personalized offers and discounts to customers, such as a favorite drink discount on their birthday or promotions based on past purchases.

- Inventory Management: By understanding customer purchasing patterns, Starbucks can better manage inventory, ensuring popular items are always in stock and reducing waste.

- Menu Optimization: Data insights help Starbucks refine its menu offerings by identifying which products are most popular and which ones are underperforming.

Amazon: Optimizing the E-commerce Experience

How They're Using Marketing Data: Amazon leverages vast amounts of marketing data to optimize its e-commerce experience. This includes data on customer searches, browsing history, purchase history, reviews, and feedback.

Benefits:

- Product Recommendations: Amazon's recommendation engine suggests products based on user behavior, leading to increased cross-selling and upselling opportunities.

- Pricing Strategy: Amazon uses data to implement dynamic pricing, adjusting prices in real-time based on demand, competitor pricing, and other factors to maximize sales and profits.

- Customer Service: Data analytics help Amazon predict and address potential customer service issues. For example, if a product is frequently returned, Amazon can investigate and address the root cause, whether it's a quality issue or misleading product descriptions.

These examples illustrate how marketing data can be used effectively to enhance customer experiences, optimize operations, and drive strategic business decisions. By leveraging data, brands like Netflix, Starbucks, and Amazon can maintain a competitive edge and foster stronger customer relationships.

By implementing these best practices, businesses can harness the power of marketing data and analytics to drive growth, enhance customer experiences, and stay ahead in a competitive market.

CHAPTER 22
Business Dashboards and Marketing KPIs

A business dashboard is a visual tool that consolidates and displays key performance indicators (KPIs), metrics, and other critical data points relevant to an organization's operations and goals. It serves as a centralized platform where stakeholders, including executives, managers, and department heads, can monitor and analyze real-time information to make informed decisions and drive business performance.

Purpose and Functionality

The primary purpose of a business dashboard is to provide a comprehensive and intuitive view of business performance. By gathering data from various sources such as CRM systems, ERP software, financial databases, and marketing platforms, dashboards present this data in visually appealing formats like charts, graphs, gauges, and tables. This visualization helps users quickly grasp trends, patterns, and anomalies, enabling them to identify areas of strength, weakness, and opportunity within the organization.

Types of Business Dashboards

Business dashboards come in several types, each serving different organizational needs:

- **Strategic Dashboards:** Focus on high-level goals and long-term objectives, providing executives with insights into overall business performance and alignment with strategic initiatives.

- **Operational Dashboards:** Monitor real-time operations and day-to-day activities such as production outputs, inventory levels, and customer service metrics, helping managers keep operations running smoothly.

- **Analytical Dashboards:** Enable in-depth analysis by allowing users to drill down into specific datasets, uncovering correlations, trends, and root causes behind performance metrics.

Benefits of Using Business Dashboards

The benefits of business dashboards extend across various aspects of organizational management:

- **Decision-Making:** Dashboards facilitate data-driven decision-making by presenting actionable insights derived from KPIs and metrics, empowering stakeholders to respond swiftly to changes and opportunities.

- **Performance Monitoring:** Real-time updates on key metrics allow for proactive management, ensuring timely interventions to address issues and capitalize on emerging trends.

- **Transparency and Accountability:** By making performance data accessible and understandable, dashboards foster transparency and accountability within the organization, promoting alignment with strategic goals.

- **Efficiency and Productivity:** Access to centralized, up-to-date information reduces the time spent on gathering and analyzing data manually, freeing up resources for more strategic tasks.

Key Components and Design Considerations

Effective business dashboards share common components and design principles:

- **Visualization:** Utilization of visual elements like color-coded charts, trend lines, and heat maps to convey complex data clearly and understandably.

- **Interactivity:** Incorporation of interactive features such as filters, drill-down capabilities, and hover-over tooltips to facilitate exploration and deeper analysis of data subsets.

- **Customization:** Ability for users to customize dashboard views based on their roles and specific information needs, ensuring relevance and usability.

- **Integration:** Seamless integration of data from multiple sources ensures a unified view of business performance while maintaining data accuracy and consistency.

Challenges and Considerations

Implementing and maintaining effective business dashboards can present challenges:

- **Data Integration:** Overcoming technical complexities associated with integrating data from disparate systems and ensuring data quality and consistency.

- **User Adoption:** Providing adequate training and support to ensure that users understand how to interpret dashboard insights and leverage them effectively.

- **Scalability:** Ensuring that dashboards can scale with the organization's growth and evolving data needs, accommodating additional data sources and expanding user base.

Dashboards and Key Performance Indicators (KPIs) are critical tools in modern marketing that help businesses track performance, make data-driven decisions, and achieve strategic goals. Here's an overview of dashboards, their importance, and how KPIs are used in marketing:

Introduction to Marketing Dashboards

Dashboards are visual representations of data that consolidate information from multiple sources into a single, easy-to-read interface. In marketing, dashboards aggregate data from various channels such as websites, social media platforms, email campaigns, and advertising campaigns. They provide real-time insights into key metrics, allowing marketers and stakeholders to monitor performance at a glance.

Types of Marketing Dashboards

Marketing dashboards can be categorized into several types based on their focus:

- Campaign Performance Dashboards: Track the effectiveness of marketing campaigns, including metrics like click-through rates, conversion rates, and ROI.

- Social Media Dashboards: Monitor engagement metrics, follower growth, content performance, and sentiment analysis across social media channels.

- SEO Dashboards: Display metrics related to organic search performance, keyword rankings, backlinks, and website traffic.

- Sales and Revenue Dashboards: Show metrics such as lead generation, sales pipeline, revenue growth, and customer acquisition costs.

Importance of Dashboards in Marketing

Dashboards play a crucial role in marketing for several reasons:

- Real-time Monitoring: Provide up-to-date information on campaign performance, enabling marketers to react quickly to changes and optimize strategies.

- Data Visualization: Present complex data in a visually appealing and understandable format, making it easier for stakeholders to grasp insights and trends.

- Performance Tracking: Track progress towards marketing goals and KPIs, helping teams stay aligned and accountable.

- Decision Making: Enable data-driven decision-making by providing insights into what is working well and where adjustments are needed.

Key Performance Indicators (KPIs) in Marketing

KPIs are quantifiable metrics used to evaluate the success of marketing activities and initiatives. They vary depending on the specific goals and objectives of each campaign or strategy. Common marketing KPIs include:

- Conversion Rate: The percentage of website visitors who complete a desired action, such as making a purchase or filling out a form.

- Customer Acquisition Cost (CAC): The average cost to acquire a new customer through marketing efforts.

- Return on Investment (ROI): The ratio of net profit to the cost of an investment, typically used to measure the profitability of marketing campaigns.

- Traffic Metrics: Metrics such as website traffic, page views, and bounce rates that indicate the effectiveness of digital marketing efforts.

- Social Media Engagement: Metrics like likes, shares, comments, and follower growth that measure audience interaction with social media content.

Selecting Relevant KPIs

Choosing the right KPIs depends on the specific goals and objectives of the marketing campaign or initiative. KPIs should be:

- Aligned with Goals: Directly related to the desired outcomes of the marketing strategy, whether it's increasing sales, improving brand awareness, or enhancing customer satisfaction.

- Measurable: Quantifiable and trackable over time to assess progress and performance.

- Actionable: Provide insights that can inform strategic decisions and optimizations.

Designing Effective Dashboards

Effective marketing dashboards are designed with usability and functionality in mind:

- Customizable Views: Allow users to customize dashboard views based on their roles and responsibilities, displaying relevant metrics and data visualizations.

- Interactive Features: Include filters, drill-down capabilities, and tooltips to enable deeper exploration of data and trends.

- Mobile Compatibility: Ensure dashboards are accessible on mobile devices, enabling marketers to monitor performance on the go.

- Data Integration: Integrate data from multiple sources seamlessly to provide a comprehensive view of marketing efforts.

Implementing Dashboards in Marketing Strategy

Integrating dashboards into the marketing strategy involves several steps:

- Identify Objectives: Define specific goals and objectives that the dashboard will help achieve, such as increasing ROI or improving campaign performance.

- Select Data Sources: Determine which data sources are relevant to track and integrate into the dashboard, ensuring data accuracy and consistency.

- Choose Visualization Tools: Select dashboard tools and software that align with the organization's needs and budget, considering factors like scalability and user interface.

- Set Up Automation: Automate data collection and updates to ensure real-time insights and minimize manual effort in maintaining the dashboard.

Monitoring and Optimization

Once implemented, marketing dashboards should be regularly monitored and optimized:

- Regular Reviews: Conduct periodic reviews of dashboard performance and data accuracy to ensure reliability and relevance.

- Performance Analysis: Analyze trends, patterns, and outliers in KPIs to identify areas for improvement and optimization.

- Benchmarking: Compare current performance against past benchmarks and industry standards to gauge progress and set new goals.

- Iterative Improvements: Continuously refine dashboard design and KPI selection based on feedback, changing business needs, and technological advancements.

Communicating Insights

Effective communication of insights derived from dashboards is crucial for driving alignment and action across the organization:

- Visual Storytelling: Use data visualizations and narratives to communicate key findings and trends to stakeholders.

- Actionable Recommendations: Translate insights into actionable recommendations and strategic initiatives that can drive business growth.

- Collaborative Approach: Foster collaboration between marketing teams, sales teams, and executives based on shared insights and data-driven decision-making.

Scaling and Adaptation

As business needs evolve, marketing dashboards should be scalable and adaptable to accommodate growth and changes in strategy:

- Scalability: Ensure the dashboard can handle increasing data volumes and complexities as the business grows.

- Adaptability: Stay agile by modifying dashboards and KPIs to reflect new marketing objectives, emerging trends, and shifts in consumer behavior.

- Continuous Learning: Embrace a culture of continuous learning and improvement, leveraging insights from dashboards to innovate and stay ahead of competitors in the dynamic marketing landscape.

Dashboards and KPIs are indispensable tools for modern marketers seeking to optimize performance, enhance decision-making, and drive business growth through data-driven insights and strategic actions. By effectively leveraging these tools, businesses can gain a competitive edge and achieve their marketing objectives more effectively.

Best Practices: Managing a Marketing Dashboard for Business

Managing a weekly marketing dashboard for digital campaigns requires careful planning, consistent monitoring, and agile decision-making to ensure effective campaign management and optimization. Here are some best practices for managing a weekly marketing dashboard:

Define Clear Objectives and KPIs: Start by defining clear objectives and key performance indicators (KPIs) that align with your digital campaign goals. These might include metrics such as website traffic, conversion rates, cost per acquisition (CPA), return on ad spend (ROAS), and engagement rates on social media platforms.

Automate Data Integration: Automate the integration of data from various digital marketing channels and platforms into your dashboard. Use tools and software that allow seamless connectivity with sources like Google Analytics, advertising platforms (e.g., Google Ads, Facebook Ads), email marketing platforms and CRM systems. This ensures that your dashboard is updated in real-time or near real-time.

Focus on Relevant Metrics: Display only the most relevant metrics and KPIs that provide actionable insights for decision-making. Avoid overwhelming the dashboard with unnecessary data points. Prioritize metrics that directly impact campaign performance and align with your strategic objectives.

Monitor Trends and Performance Changes: Regularly monitor trends and changes in key metrics week over week. Use visualizations such as line charts, bar graphs, and trend lines to track performance trends and identify anomalies or fluctuations that may require attention. Compare current performance against historical data to gauge progress and identify areas for improvement.

Implement Filters and Drill-Down Capabilities: Incorporate interactive features like filters, drill-down capabilities, and segmentation options in your dashboard. This allows users to explore data at a more granular level, such as by campaign, channel, audience segment, or geographic region. These features enable deeper analysis and help uncover insights that can inform optimization strategies.

Set Up Alerts and Notifications: Configure alerts and notifications within the dashboard to highlight significant changes or deviations from expected performance metrics. Alerts can notify stakeholders of sudden drops in conversion rates, spikes in ad spend, or other critical events that require immediate attention. This proactive approach helps in timely troubleshooting and course correction.

Collaborate and Share Insights: Use the dashboard as a centralized tool for collaboration among marketing teams, executives, and other stakeholders. Share insights and findings from the dashboard during regular meetings or through collaborative platforms. Encourage discussion around performance trends, successes, challenges, and action plans for optimization.

Review and Optimize Campaign Strategies: Use insights gained from the dashboard to review and optimize digital campaign strategies on a weekly basis. Identify underperforming campaigns or channels and allocate resources accordingly. Adjust targeting parameters, creative elements, budget allocations, and bidding strategies based on data-driven insights to maximize ROI and achieve campaign objectives.

A PRACTICAL GUIDE TO DIGITAL MARKETING

By adhering to these best practices, businesses can effectively manage their weekly marketing dashboards for digital campaigns, enabling agile decision-making, continuous optimization, and ultimately, driving success in their digital marketing efforts.

CHAPTER 23
Public Relations in a Digital World

Public Relations (PR) is the strategic communication efforts undertaken by organizations or individuals to build and maintain a favorable public image and reputation. It involves managing the spread of information between an organization and its target audience, including customers, stakeholders, investors, employees, and the general public. PR aims to create a positive perception of the organization, enhance its credibility, and cultivate goodwill.

Key Functions of Public Relations:

Building Relationships: PR professionals focus on establishing and nurturing relationships with various stakeholders, including media representatives, influencers, community leaders, and industry partners. These relationships are crucial for disseminating positive messages and managing crises effectively.

Media Relations: Managing media relations is a core component of PR. This involves cultivating contacts with journalists, editors, and bloggers to secure media coverage and positive publicity for the organization. PR professionals draft press releases, organize press conferences, and respond to media inquiries to ensure accurate and favorable media coverage.

Reputation Management: PR plays a critical role in safeguarding and enhancing the organization's reputation. PR professionals monitor public sentiment, address negative perceptions or misconceptions, and implement strategies to mitigate reputation risks. They also promote the organization's achievements, initiatives, and corporate social responsibility efforts to build trust and credibility.

Crisis Communication: During crises or challenging situations, PR professionals develop and execute crisis communication plans to manage public perception and minimize reputational damage. They provide timely and transparent information, address concerns, and demonstrate accountability to stakeholders.

Strategic Communication: PR involves developing and executing strategic communication campaigns aligned with the organization's goals and objectives. This includes promoting new product launches, corporate milestones, industry partnerships, and thought leadership initiatives through various communication channels.

Tools and Techniques Used in Public Relations:

- Media Relations: Press releases, media pitches, interviews, and media training.

- Digital PR: Leveraging digital platforms, social media, and online channels to reach and engage with target audiences.

- Events and Sponsorships: Organizing events, sponsoring industry conferences, and participating in community outreach programs.

- Content Creation: Developing compelling content such as articles, blogs, newsletters, and whitepapers to educate and inform stakeholders.

- Influencer Relations: Collaborating with industry influencers and thought leaders to amplify brand messages and reach new audiences.

- Internal Communications: Engaging and informing employees through internal newsletters, town hall meetings, and intranet updates.

Importance of Public Relations:

Public relations (PR) plays a vital role in helping businesses build and maintain a positive public image, engage with stakeholders, and achieve their strategic goals. Here are five compelling reasons why businesses should invest in public relations:

Enhancing Credibility and Trust: PR helps businesses establish credibility and build trust among key stakeholders, including customers, investors, employees, and the general public. By effectively communicating the organization's values, achievements, and commitment to ethical practices through media coverage, press releases, and other PR tactics, businesses can strengthen their reputation and foster trust.

Managing Reputation and Perception: Reputation management is a cornerstone of PR. In today's digital age, where information spreads rapidly, businesses must actively manage their reputation to safeguard against negative publicity and crises. PR professionals monitor public sentiment, address misconceptions or controversies, and promote positive news to shape public perception and maintain a favorable reputation.

Driving Brand Awareness and Visibility: PR initiatives help businesses increase brand awareness and visibility in the marketplace. By securing media coverage in industry events and leveraging digital PR strategies such as social media and content marketing, businesses can reach a broader audience and attract potential customers. Consistent PR efforts ensure that the brand remains top-of-mind among target audiences.

Supporting Marketing and Sales Efforts: Public relations complements marketing and sales strategies by generating publicity and creating opportunities for lead generation. PR campaigns can highlight product launches, customer success stories, and industry accolades, effectively influencing purchasing decisions and driving sales. By positioning the brand positively in the media and marketplace, PR contributes to overall marketing effectiveness.

Engaging with Stakeholders and Influencers: PR facilitates meaningful engagement with stakeholders, including customers, industry influencers, community leaders, and government officials. Through media relations, social media engagement, and corporate events, businesses can foster relationships, solicit feedback, and gain valuable insights into market trends and customer preferences. Engaged stakeholders are more likely to advocate for the brand and support its growth initiatives.

Public relations is essential for businesses seeking to build credibility, manage reputation, enhance brand visibility, support marketing efforts, and engage effectively with stakeholders. By investing in strategic PR initiatives, businesses can cultivate a positive public image, strengthen relationships, and achieve long-term success in today's competitive marketplace.

Public Relations has Changed in the Digital Word.

Public relations (PR) has undergone significant transformation in the digital era, driven by advancements in technology, shifts in consumer behavior, and the evolution of communication channels. Here are several ways in which public relations has changed in the digital world:

Instantaneous Communication: Digital platforms such as social media, blogs, and news websites enable instant and direct communication between organizations and their audiences. PR professionals can disseminate information rapidly, respond to inquiries in real time, and engage in two-way conversations with stakeholders.

Expanded Reach and Targeting: Digital PR allows businesses to reach global audiences more effectively than traditional methods. Through online publications, social media influencers, and search engine optimization (SEO), PR campaigns can target specific demographics, interests, and geographic locations with precision.

Data-Driven Insights: Digital PR provides access to vast amounts of data and analytics, allowing PR professionals to measure campaign effectiveness, track audience engagement, and refine strategies based on actionable insights. Metrics such as website traffic, social media interactions, and conversion rates help optimize PR efforts for better results.

Content Creation and Distribution: Content lies at the heart of digital PR strategies. PR professionals create compelling content such as press releases, blogs, videos, and infographics to engage audiences across various digital channels. Content distribution through owned media (websites, blogs), earned media (press coverage), and shared media (social networks) amplifies reach and influence.

24/7 News Cycle and Crisis Management: The digital landscape operates on a continuous news cycle, where information spreads rapidly and unpredictably. PR teams must monitor online conversations, address issues promptly, and manage crises effectively to protect brand reputation.

Social media listening tools and crisis communication plans are essential in mitigating negative publicity.

Influencer and Community Engagement: Digital PR leverages influencers, bloggers, and online communities to amplify brand messages and reach niche audiences. Collaborating with influencers who have large followings can enhance brand credibility and foster authentic connections with consumers.

Interactive and Engaging Campaigns: Digital PR encourages interactive and immersive campaigns that encourage audience participation and engagement. Contests, polls, live streams, and user-generated content campaigns invite audience interaction, strengthen brand loyalty, and increase brand advocacy.

Integration with Marketing and SEO: Digital PR is closely integrated with marketing strategies and SEO practices. PR activities contribute to brand positioning, drive website traffic, and improve search engine rankings through backlinks and keyword optimization. Collaborative efforts between PR, marketing, and SEO teams ensure cohesive messaging and maximize impact.

In essence, digital PR has revolutionized the way organizations communicate, engage with audiences, and manage their reputations in the digital age. By embracing digital tools and strategies, PR professionals can adapt to evolving trends, navigate complex media landscapes, and drive meaningful connections with stakeholders to achieve business objectives.

Best Practices: Public Relations in the Digital Word

In the digital world, public relations (PR) professionals must adapt their strategies to effectively engage with audiences, manage reputations, and achieve organizational goals. Here are some best practices for public relations in the digital era:

Embrace Multi-Channel Communication: Utilize a variety of digital channels such as social media platforms (Twitter, Facebook, LinkedIn, Instagram), blogs, online news portals, and email newsletters to reach diverse audiences. Tailor messages for each platform while maintaining a consistent brand voice across all channels.

Create Engaging Content: Develop high-quality, relevant content that resonates with your target audience. This includes press releases, blog posts, articles, infographics, videos, and podcasts. Use storytelling techniques to humanize your brand and capture attention.

Build Relationships with Digital Influencers: Collaborate with influencers and thought leaders in your industry to amplify your message and reach new audiences. Identify influencers whose values align with your brand and cultivate authentic partnerships through sponsored content, guest posts, or joint campaigns.

Monitor Online Conversations: Implement social listening tools to monitor mentions, sentiment, and trends related to your brand or industry. Stay proactive in addressing customer feedback, comments, and inquiries across social media platforms. Respond promptly and transparently to maintain trust and credibility.

Optimize for Search Engines (SEO): Incorporate SEO best practices into your digital PR efforts to improve visibility and organic search rankings. Use relevant keywords, optimize meta tags, and earn backlinks from reputable websites through earned media coverage. Regularly update content to align with SEO trends and algorithms.

Measure and Analyze Performance: Use data analytics tools to track the impact of your PR campaigns and initiatives. Measure key performance indicators (KPIs) such as website traffic, social media engagement, media mentions, and sentiment analysis. Evaluate the ROI of PR activities to refine strategies and allocate resources effectively.

Stay Agile and Responsive: Adapt quickly to emerging trends, industry developments, and current events that may impact your brand or industry. Develop agile PR strategies that allow for rapid responses to opportunities and challenges in the digital landscape.

Integrate PR with Marketing and Sales: Collaborate closely with marketing and sales teams to align PR efforts with overall business objectives. Coordinate campaigns, promotions, and product launches to ensure consistent messaging and maximize impact across all customer touchpoints.

Maintain Transparency and Authenticity: Build trust with stakeholders by maintaining transparency in communications and upholding ethical standards. Avoid misleading or deceptive practices that could damage your brand reputation in the digital age of heightened scrutiny.

Continuous Learning and Adaptation: Stay informed about new technologies, tools, and trends shaping the digital PR landscape. Invest in professional development, attend industry conferences, and participate in online forums to exchange insights and best practices with peers.

By implementing these best practices, PR professionals can effectively navigate the complexities of the digital world, enhance brand visibility, foster meaningful relationships with stakeholders, and drive long-term success for their organizations.

Here are three examples of how to leverage public relations activities in business.

Content Creation and Distribution: Businesses can leverage PR by creating compelling content such as press releases, blogs, articles, infographics, and videos that highlight their expertise, achievements, and industry insights. Distributing this content through owned media channels (company website, blog), earned media (media coverage), and shared media (social media platforms) helps amplify brand messaging, engage audiences, and attract media attention.

Influencer and Media Relations: Cultivating relationships with industry influencers, bloggers, journalists, and media outlets is essential for businesses seeking to increase visibility and credibility. PR professionals can collaborate with influencers to endorse products, host sponsored content, or participate in influencer marketing campaigns. Building strong media relations involves pitching relevant stories, providing exclusive access, and responding promptly to media inquiries to secure positive press coverage and enhance brand reputation.

Event Sponsorships and Speaking Engagements: Businesses can leverage PR by sponsoring industry events, conferences, or trade shows relevant to their target audience. Sponsorship opportunities provide exposure, networking opportunities, and brand recognition among attendees. Additionally, securing speaking engagements for company executives or subject matter experts positions them as thought leaders, allowing them to share insights, showcase expertise, and build credibility within the industry.

Community Engagement and Corporate Social Responsibility (CSR): Engaging in CSR initiatives and community outreach programs demonstrates a business's commitment to social responsibility and strengthens its reputation. PR efforts can highlight charitable partnerships, volunteer activities, environmental sustainability initiatives, or philanthropic contributions through media campaigns, press releases, and social media content. By aligning corporate values with community needs, businesses can foster goodwill, enhance brand loyalty, and build positive relationships with stakeholders.

Digital and Social Media Strategy: Leveraging digital PR tactics, businesses can optimize their online presence and engage audiences through social media platforms, content marketing, and digital storytelling. PR professionals use social media channels to share company news, interact with followers, and respond to customer feedback in real-time. Implementing SEO strategies, monitoring online conversations, and utilizing analytics tools help measure PR campaign effectiveness, track engagement metrics, and adjust strategies to maximize reach and impact.

These examples demonstrate how businesses can strategically leverage public relations activities to build brand awareness, manage reputation, engage stakeholders, and drive business growth in competitive markets.

CHAPTER 24
Understanding Marketing Automation Framework

Marketing Automation

Marketing automation refers to the use of software platforms and technologies to automate repetitive tasks and workflows in marketing activities. It allows businesses to streamline, measure, and optimize marketing tasks and processes, ultimately increasing efficiency and effectiveness. Here are key aspects of marketing automation:

Automated Campaign Management: Marketing automation enables businesses to automate the management and execution of marketing campaigns across multiple channels. This includes email marketing, social media marketing, lead nurturing, customer segmentation, and more. Automated workflows can be set up to trigger actions based on customer behavior, interactions, or predefined criteria, such as sending personalized emails or messages at specific stages of the customer journey.

Lead Management and Nurturing: Marketing automation platforms facilitate lead management by capturing, tracking, and qualifying leads through various stages of the sales funnel. Leads are scored based on their engagement levels, demographics, and behaviors, allowing marketers to prioritize and nurture high-quality leads effectively. Automated workflows can deliver relevant content, follow-up messages, or alerts to sales teams when leads reach specific milestones or criteria.

Personalization and Customer Segmentation: One of the strengths of marketing automation is its ability to personalize marketing efforts at scale. Businesses can segment their audience based on demographic data, interests, purchase history, or engagement levels. Automated campaigns can then deliver targeted messages, offers, and content that resonate with each segment, increasing relevance and improving the overall customer experience.

Behavioral Tracking and Analytics: Marketing automation tools track and analyze customer behavior and interactions across digital channels in real-time. This includes website visits, email opens, click-through rates, social media engagement, and more. By capturing this data, marketers gain valuable insights into customer preferences, interests, and buying patterns, which can inform future marketing strategies and optimizations.

Cross-Channel Integration: Modern marketing automation platforms integrate seamlessly with other business systems and marketing tools, such as customer relationship management (CRM) software, content management systems (CMS), and analytics platforms. This integration allows for a holistic view of customer data and enables coordinated marketing efforts across multiple channels, ensuring consistent messaging and a unified customer experience.

Campaign Measurement and Optimization: Marketing automation provides robust analytics and reporting capabilities to measure the performance and ROI of marketing campaigns. Marketers can track key metrics such as conversion rates, lead generation, engagement rates, and revenue attribution. Insights gained from analytics help identify successful strategies, areas for improvement, and opportunities for optimization to drive continuous campaign refinement.

Efficiency and Scalability: By automating repetitive tasks, workflows, and communications, marketing automation improves operational efficiency and frees up marketers' time to focus on strategic activities. It allows businesses to scale their marketing efforts without proportional increases in resources, enabling them to reach a larger audience and drive growth more effectively.

Marketing automation empowers businesses to automate, streamline, and optimize their marketing efforts across various channels. By leveraging technology to deliver personalized experiences, nurture leads, and measure campaign performance, businesses can enhance customer engagement, drive conversions, and achieve their marketing goals more efficiently in today's digital landscape.

Resources Required To Manage Marketing Automation in Business

Implementing and managing marketing automation in business requires various resources to ensure successful deployment and ongoing effectiveness. Here are the key resources needed:

Technology Platform: Invest in a robust marketing automation platform that aligns with your business needs and goals. Choose a platform that offers features such as email marketing automation, lead management, CRM integration, analytics, and workflow automation. Popular platforms include HubSpot, Marketo, Pardot, and Mailchimp.

Skilled Team: Build a team with the necessary skills to implement and manage marketing automation. This includes marketers who understand digital marketing strategies, CRM systems, and automation tools. Additionally, having team members with analytical skills for interpreting data and optimizing campaigns is crucial.

Content Creation: Effective marketing automation relies on high-quality content. Allocate resources for creating compelling content such as emails, blog posts, landing pages, eBooks, and webinars. Content should be tailored to different stages of the buyer's journey and segmented audience groups.

CRM Integration: Integrate your marketing automation platform with your CRM system to ensure seamless data flow between marketing and sales teams. This integration allows for effective lead management, tracking customer interactions, and aligning marketing efforts with sales objectives.

Data Management and Analytics: Ensure access to reliable data management and analytics tools. Marketing automation requires accurate data for segmenting audiences, tracking campaign performance, and making data-driven decisions. Invest in tools for data collection, analysis, reporting, and visualization.

Training and Education: Provide training and ongoing education for your marketing team on how to effectively use the marketing automation platform. Training should cover platform features, best practices for campaign execution, lead nurturing strategies, A/B testing, and interpreting analytics.

Budget Allocation: Allocate the budget for investing in marketing automation software licenses, CRM integration costs, content creation, data management tools, and ongoing platform support. Consider both initial setup costs and recurring expenses for maintaining and optimizing automation processes.

Customer Support and Consultation: Utilize customer support resources provided by your automation platform provider. This includes technical support, troubleshooting assistance, and access to customer success managers for guidance on platform usage, best practices, and resolving issues.

Compliance and Security: Ensure compliance with data protection regulations (e.g., GDPR, CCPA) when collecting, storing, and using customer data within your automation platform. Allocate resources for implementing security measures to protect sensitive information and build trust with your audience.

Continuous Improvement: Dedicate resources to continuously monitor, analyze, and optimize your marketing automation efforts. This includes conducting regular audits of campaigns, testing new strategies, refining workflows based on performance data, and staying updated with industry trends and platform updates.

By leveraging these resources effectively, businesses can implement and manage marketing automation to streamline processes, enhance customer engagement, drive conversions, and achieve sustainable growth in their digital marketing initiatives.

Here are three examples of businesses leveraging marketing automation along with the benefits they derive.

Mailchimp: Use of Marketing Automation: Mailchimp, an email marketing platform, offers robust marketing automation features. Businesses can set up automated email campaigns triggered by user actions such as sign-ups, purchases, or abandoned carts. They also provide personalized recommendations based on user behavior.

Benefits:

- o **Increased Efficiency:** Saves time by automating repetitive tasks like email follow-ups and customer segmentation.

- o **Improved Engagement:** Sends targeted messages based on user behavior, increasing open rates and click-through rates.

- o **Higher Conversions:** Nurtures leads with relevant content, leading to higher conversion rates and improved ROI.

Salesforce: Use of Marketing Automation: Salesforce integrates marketing automation into its CRM platform. Businesses can automate lead nurturing, send personalized emails, and track customer interactions across multiple channels. Automated workflows help in managing customer journeys from lead generation to conversion.

Benefits:

- o **Enhanced Lead Management:** Streamlines lead scoring and qualification processes, ensuring sales teams focus on the most promising leads.

- o **Improved Sales and Marketing Alignment:** Facilitates seamless communication between sales and marketing teams, leading to better collaboration and alignment of goals.

- o **Data-Driven Insights:** Provides actionable insights through analytics and reporting, enabling businesses to optimize campaigns and drive revenue growth.

HubSpot: Use of Marketing Automation: HubSpot offers a comprehensive marketing automation platform that includes email marketing, lead management, social media scheduling, and analytics. Businesses can automate workflows, segment contacts based on behavior, and personalize communications to nurture leads and drive conversions.

Benefits:

- o Personalized Customer Experiences: Delivers targeted content and offers based on customer preferences and interactions, enhancing engagement and satisfaction.

- o Scalability: Allows businesses to scale marketing efforts efficiently without increasing resource allocation proportionately.

- o Measurable ROI: Tracks campaign performance and ROI metrics in real-time, enabling continuous optimization of marketing strategies for better results.

These examples illustrate how businesses across different sectors leverage marketing automation to streamline operations, enhance customer relationships, and achieve measurable business outcomes. By automating repetitive tasks, personalizing customer interactions, and optimizing marketing efforts, businesses can achieve higher efficiency, scalability, and, ultimately, greater business success.

CHAPTER 25
Data Protection and Data Privacy Strategies

Data protection and privacy strategies are critical in today's digital world to safeguard personal and sensitive information from unauthorized access, breaches, and misuse. Here are key aspects and strategies businesses should consider:

Data Encryption: Encrypting sensitive data both at rest and in transit ensures that even if data is intercepted or accessed without authorization, it remains unreadable and unusable to unauthorized parties. Implementing strong encryption algorithms helps protect data integrity and confidentiality.

Access Control: Limiting access to sensitive data based on the principle of least privilege ensures that only authorized individuals or systems can access specific data. Implementing role-based access controls (RBAC) and regularly reviewing access permissions helps mitigate the risk of insider threats and unauthorized access.

Data Minimization: Collecting and retaining only necessary data reduces the risk associated with storing excessive or irrelevant information. Implement policies and procedures that govern data collection, retention periods, and deletion to minimize exposure to data breaches and regulatory scrutiny.

User Consent and Transparency: Obtaining explicit consent from individuals before collecting and processing their personal data builds trust and ensures compliance with data protection regulations such as GDPR (General Data Protection Regulation) and CCPA (California Consumer Privacy Act). Providing transparent information about data practices, including purposes of data processing and data sharing practices, enhances transparency and accountability.

Data Breach Response Plan: Developing and implementing a data breach response plan outlines steps to detect, respond to, and mitigate the impact of data breaches promptly. This includes conducting regular risk assessments, establishing incident response teams, and communicating breach notifications to affected individuals and regulatory authorities as required by law.

Data Privacy by Design and Default: Integrating data privacy principles into the design and development of systems, products, and services ensures that privacy considerations are addressed from the outset. Implementing measures such as anonymization, pseudonymization, and privacy-enhancing technologies (PETs) helps protect individual privacy while achieving business objectives.

Regular Security Audits and Assessments: Conducting regular security audits and assessments helps identify vulnerabilities, gaps in data protection measures, and compliance with regulatory requirements. Performing penetration testing, vulnerability scanning, and security assessments ensures continuous improvement of data protection practices.

Employee Training and Awareness: Educating employees about data protection policies, best practices, and regulatory requirements reduces the risk of human errors and insider threats. Regular training programs on data handling, phishing awareness, and incident reporting empower employees to contribute to the organization's overall data protection efforts.

Vendor Management: Implementing robust vendor management practices ensures that third-party vendors and service providers comply with data protection requirements. Establishing contractual agreements, conducting due diligence assessments, and monitoring vendor compliance with security and privacy standards mitigate risks associated with outsourcing data processing activities.

Compliance Monitoring and Reporting: Establishing mechanisms to monitor compliance with data protection regulations and internal policies helps demonstrate accountability and adherence to legal requirements. Maintaining detailed records of data processing activities, conducting privacy impact assessments (PIAs), and preparing for regulatory audits facilitate compliance and minimize legal and reputational risks.

Effective data protection and privacy strategies involve implementing technical, organizational, and procedural measures to safeguard personal data, uphold individual rights, and maintain trust in the digital economy. Businesses that prioritize data protection as part of their core values and operational practices are better positioned to mitigate risks, enhance customer confidence, and achieve sustainable growth in an increasingly data-driven world.

Resources Needed To Managing Data Protection and Privacy

Managing data protection and privacy strategies effectively requires various resources to ensure compliance, mitigate risks, and safeguard sensitive information. Here are essential resources businesses need:

Dedicated Data Protection Officer (DPO): Appointing a DPO or a designated privacy officer responsible for overseeing data protection and privacy initiatives is crucial. The DPO ensures compliance with data protection regulations, develops and implements privacy policies and procedures, and serves as a point of contact for data subjects and regulatory authorities.

Comprehensive Data Protection Policies and Procedures: Developing and maintaining clear and comprehensive data protection policies and procedures that outline how personal data is collected, processed, stored, and shared. These policies should align with regulatory requirements such as GDPR, CCPA, and other relevant data protection laws.

Data Protection Impact Assessments (DPIAs): Conducting DPIAs to assess and mitigate privacy risks associated with data processing activities. DPIAs help identify potential privacy impacts, evaluate the necessity and proportionality of data processing, and implement measures to minimize risks to data subjects.

Data Protection Training and Awareness Programs: Providing regular training and awareness programs for employees to educate them about data protection principles, organizational policies, and compliance requirements. Training programs should cover topics such as data handling practices, secure data storage, incident response procedures, and recognizing phishing attempts.

Privacy-Enhancing Technologies (PETs): Investing in and implementing privacy-enhancing technologies such as encryption, anonymization, pseudonymization, and data masking solutions. PETs help protect sensitive data from unauthorized access, enhance data privacy by design, and mitigate risks associated with data breaches.

Data Breach Response Plan: Developing and maintaining a data breach response plan that outlines steps to detect, respond to, and mitigate the impact of data breaches. The plan should include procedures for assessing the severity of breaches, notifying affected individuals and regulatory authorities, and conducting post-incident reviews to prevent future incidents.

Legal and Regulatory Expertise: Access to legal counsel or compliance experts with expertise in data protection laws and regulations applicable to your business operations. Legal advisors help interpret regulatory requirements, provide guidance on compliance strategies, and assist in responding to regulatory inquiries or investigations.

Data Governance Framework: Implementing a data governance framework that defines roles, responsibilities, and accountability for data protection within the organization. A governance framework ensures that data protection policies are integrated into business processes, IT systems, and organizational culture.

Regular Compliance Audits and Assessments: Conduct regular compliance audits and assessments to evaluate the effectiveness of data protection measures, identify gaps or vulnerabilities, and address non-compliance issues proactively. Audits help maintain regulatory compliance, demonstrate accountability, and strengthen data protection practices over time.

By allocating resources to these essential components, businesses can effectively manage data protection and privacy strategies, uphold individual rights, mitigate risks associated with data breaches, and maintain trust and confidence among customers, employees, and stakeholders.

CHAPTER 26
New Emerging Technology & Platforms

Here are some new technologies and trends in digital marketing that are shaping the industry:

Artificial Intelligence (AI) and Machine Learning: AI and machine learning are transforming digital marketing by enabling personalized customer experiences, predictive analytics, and automation of repetitive tasks. AI-powered chatbots, recommendation engines, and content-generation tools help businesses enhance customer engagement and operational efficiency.

Voice Search Optimization: With the rise of voice-activated devices like smart speakers and virtual assistants (e.g., Siri, Alexa), optimizing content for voice search has become crucial. Marketers are adapting SEO strategies to focus on long-tail keywords, natural language queries, and local search optimization to capture voice search traffic.

Augmented Reality (AR) and Virtual Reality (VR): AR and VR technologies are revolutionizing digital marketing by offering immersive brand experiences. Businesses use AR for virtual try-on experiences, interactive product demos, and location-based AR campaigns. VR is used for virtual tours, immersive storytelling, and engaging virtual events.

Programmatic Advertising: Programmatic advertising leverages AI and real-time bidding (RTB) to automate the buying and placement of digital ads across websites, social media platforms, and mobile apps. Marketers use programmatic platforms to target specific audiences, optimize ad placements, and maximize return on ad spend (ROAS).

Video Marketing Dominance: Video continues to dominate digital marketing strategies due to its high engagement and storytelling capabilities. Live streaming, interactive videos, and shoppable videos are gaining popularity. Platforms like YouTube, TikTok, and Instagram Reels are key channels for video content distribution.

Data Privacy and Compliance: With increasing data privacy regulations (e.g., GDPR, CCPA), businesses are prioritizing data protection and compliance. Transparent data collection practices, user consent management, and robust data security measures are essential for maintaining consumer trust and regulatory compliance.

Social Commerce and Influencer Marketing: Social commerce integrates e-commerce functionalities into social media platforms, allowing users to shop directly from social posts and ads. Influencer marketing remains effective, with brands collaborating with influencers to reach targeted audiences authentically and drive purchase decisions.

Chatbots and Conversational Marketing: Chatbots powered by AI are used for real-time customer support, lead generation, and personalized recommendations. Conversational marketing strategies involve using chatbots and messaging apps to engage prospects, qualify leads, and deliver personalized customer experiences.

Customer Data Platforms (CDPs): CDPs consolidate customer data from multiple sources into a single unified profile. Marketers use CDPs to gain insights into customer behavior, create personalized marketing campaigns across channels, and measure campaign effectiveness based on unified data analytics.

Blockchain Technology in Digital Advertising: Blockchain is increasingly used to enhance transparency, combat ad fraud, and verify digital ad impressions and transactions. Blockchain-powered solutions offer decentralized ad networks, secure data sharing, and enhanced trust between advertisers, publishers, and consumers.

These technologies and trends highlight the evolving landscape of digital marketing, emphasizing innovation, personalization, and the importance of data-driven strategies in achieving marketing objectives and driving business growth.

Below are examples that illustrate how new technologies and trends in digital marketing are reshaping strategies, enhancing customer engagement, and driving measurable results for businesses across various industries:

Artificial Intelligence (AI) and Machine Learning

- **Chatbots:** AI-powered chatbots offer 24/7 customer support, handle inquiries, and guide users through sales funnels without human intervention. Examples include chatbots on websites like Drift and Intercom.

- **Predictive Analytics:** Machine learning algorithms analyze large datasets to predict customer behavior, optimize ad targeting, and personalize content. Platforms like Google Analytics and Salesforce Einstein use predictive analytics to forecast trends and optimize marketing strategies.

- **Content Generation:** AI tools like Copy.ai and Conversion.ai generate engaging content, including blog posts, ad copy, and social media captions, based on user inputs and data insights.

Voice Search Optimization

- **Natural Language Processing (NLP):** NLP technologies understand and process natural language queries, optimizing content for voice search. Examples include optimizing content with long-tail keywords and conversational phrases.

- **Voice-Activated Devices:** Devices like Amazon Echo (Alexa), Google Home, and Apple HomePod enable users to search and shop using voice commands, driving the need for voice-optimized content and SEO strategies.

- **Featured Snippets and Position Zero:** Voice search often pulls responses from featured snippets, so optimizing content to appear in position zero on search engine results pages (SERPs) improves visibility for voice queries.

Augmented Reality (AR) and Virtual Reality (VR)

- **Virtual Try-Ons:** Retailers use AR technology for virtual try-ons, allowing customers to visualize products (e.g., clothing, makeup) before purchase. Examples include Sephora's Virtual Artist and IKEA Place.

- **AR Advertising:** Brands integrate AR elements into advertising campaigns to create interactive and immersive experiences. For instance, Coca-Cola's AR campaign during the FIFA World Cup allowed users to play virtual soccer games using their mobile devices.

- **Virtual Events and Tours:** VR technology enables virtual tours of real estate properties, tourist destinations, and event venues. Platforms like Oculus Rift and HTC Vive offer immersive experiences for virtual conferences and exhibitions.

Programmatic Advertising

- **Real-Time Bidding (RTB):** Programmatic platforms like Google Ads and DSPs (Demand-Side Platforms) automate ad buying and placement in real-time auctions, optimizing bids based on targeting criteria and campaign goals.

- **Audience Targeting:** Marketers use programmatic advertising to target specific audience segments based on demographics, behaviors, and interests across display, video, and mobile ad inventory.

- **Dynamic Creative Optimization (DCO):** DCO personalizes ad creative in real-time based on user data such as location, device type, and browsing history. Advertisers use platforms like Adobe Advertising Cloud and The Trade Desk for DCO campaigns.

CHAPTER 27
Conclusion

As businesses embark on transforming their operations and leveraging digital marketing, several critical considerations emerge to ensure a successful and impactful transition:

Alignment with Strategic Objectives: Aligning digital marketing efforts with overarching business goals is paramount. Whether the focus is on expanding market share, improving customer retention, or launching new products/services, every digital initiative should tie back to these strategic objectives. This alignment ensures that resources are effectively allocated, and efforts contribute directly to business growth.

Customer-Centric Approach: Adopting a customer-centric approach is essential in today's digital landscape. Understanding customer preferences, behaviors, and pain points through data analytics and market research allows businesses to tailor their digital marketing strategies accordingly. Personalization becomes key, enabling businesses to deliver relevant content, offers, and experiences that resonate with their target audience.

Omnichannel Integration: Embracing an omnichannel strategy ensures a cohesive brand experience across multiple touchpoints. Integrating digital channels such as social media, email marketing, websites, mobile apps, and offline interactions provides customers with seamless interactions and consistent messaging. This approach not only enhances customer engagement but also strengthens brand loyalty and increases conversion rates.

A PRACTICAL GUIDE TO DIGITAL MARKETING

Data-Driven Decision-Making: Leveraging data analytics to drive decision-making processes is critical for optimizing digital marketing efforts. By analyzing key performance indicators (KPIs) such as website traffic, conversion rates, customer acquisition costs, and ROI, businesses can gain actionable insights. These insights inform campaign adjustments, content optimizations, and resource allocations, ultimately improving campaign effectiveness and efficiency.

Agility and Adaptability: Remaining agile and adaptable in response to market trends, consumer behavior shifts, and technological advancements is essential. Digital marketing landscapes evolve rapidly, necessitating businesses to continuously innovate and iterate their strategies. Flexibility in testing new tactics, embracing emerging technologies (e.g., AI, AR/VR), and adjusting campaigns based on performance metrics enables businesses to stay competitive and relevant.

Compliance and Ethical Considerations: Upholding data privacy regulations (e.g., GDPR, CCPA) and maintaining ethical standards in digital marketing practices are non-negotiable. Businesses must prioritize consumer trust and transparency by obtaining consent for data collection and usage, safeguarding sensitive information, and adhering to industry guidelines. This commitment to ethical conduct not only mitigates legal risks but also fosters long-term customer relationships built on trust.

Investment in Talent and Training: Investing in a skilled workforce equipped with digital marketing expertise is crucial. Providing ongoing training and professional development opportunities ensures that team members stay abreast of industry trends, best practices, and technological advancements. Empowered employees can effectively execute digital strategies, innovate creatively, and drive organizational growth through their specialized knowledge.

Collaboration and Partnerships: Collaborating with external partners, agencies, or industry influencers can amplify digital marketing efforts. Strategic partnerships enable access to specialized expertise, broader audience reach, and innovative campaign ideas. Whether through co-marketing initiatives, influencer collaborations, or joint ventures, partnerships can accelerate growth and enhance brand visibility in competitive markets.

Continuous Optimization and Innovation: Adopting a culture of continuous improvement is crucial for optimizing digital marketing performance. Implementing A/B testing, analyzing performance metrics, and iterating based on insights allow businesses to refine campaigns and maximize ROI. Embracing innovation by exploring new technologies, experimenting with creative formats, and anticipating industry shifts positions businesses as industry leaders and innovators.

Risk Management and Resilience: Proactively managing risks associated with digital marketing, such as cybersecurity threats, algorithm updates, or economic downturns, is essential for business resilience. Developing contingency plans, diversifying marketing channels, and maintaining financial stability mitigate potential disruptions and ensure continuity in achieving strategic objectives.

In summary, successful transformation and effective utilization of digital marketing require a holistic approach that integrates strategic alignment, customer-centricity, data-driven insights, agility, compliance, talent investment, collaboration, continuous optimization, and risk management. By prioritizing these considerations, businesses can navigate digital landscapes with confidence, drive sustainable growth, and build enduring competitive advantages in their respective industries.

About The Author

Sebastian Pistritto, chief marketing officer with over 25 years of multichannel marketing communication, business development and technical Product Management experience in both a Vice President and a Director role. Pistritto provides thought leadership on digital and multichannel marketing programs. Experience in such industries as technology, health care, retail, automotive, financial, software and consumer electronics. I have served as the Chief Marketing Officer for several organizations, responsible for marketing communications, brand management, and strategy. Sebastian is an experienced enterprise software marketing executive with years of experience developing go-to-market strategies and brand narratives, building high-performance teams, and driving demand generation.

Chief Marketing Officer with experience with high-growth companies in healthcare, fintech, technology, automotive, retail, consumer marketing and financial services.

Over my career, I have been responsible for the following:

* Develop and execute comprehensive marketing strategies to drive customer acquisition, retention, and engagement.

* Lead a team of marketing professionals, providing guidance, mentorship, and support to ensure the successful implementation of marketing plans.

* Use market research and analysis to identify trends, insights, and opportunities and translate them into actionable marketing strategies.

* Collaborate with product management, sales, and other cross-functional teams to develop integrated marketing strategies and briefs that align with business objectives.

* Oversee the development and execution of multi-channel marketing campaigns, including digital marketing, social media, email marketing, content marketing, and traditional advertising.

* Drive brand awareness and recognition through effective messaging, storytelling, and creative campaigns.

* Partner with marketing leaders to monitor and analyze marketing campaign performance, track key performance indicators (KPIs), and make data-driven decisions to optimize marketing efforts and maximize ROI.

* Stay abreast of industry trends, emerging technologies, and best practices in consumer marketing to identify new opportunities for growth and innovation.

* Manage marketing budgets, allocate resources effectively, and ensure cost-effective marketing campaigns.

Pistritto has published numerous articles, including: 7 Steps on Engaging with Mobile Consumers, Selecting an Adserver Technology, and Managing Your Lead Qualification Process, which have appeared in Internet.com, Mobile Marketer, MicroStation Manager Magazine, CtrlAltDelete Newsletter, VARiety Newsletter, InView Newsletter, and Insider Reports Journal. Pistritto is a recipient of the 2000 Distinguished Technical Communication Award from the Society for Technical Communication.

Pistritto has presented at a number of industry events such as: Consumer Electronic Show (CES), Storage Visions-Home Network, Intel Developer Forum, CEATEC JAPAN and Fall Focus: On-demand Digital Entertainment conference.

Pistritto brings marketing leadership experience and a proven track record of driving transformative growth. He holds a Bachelor of Science in Business Administration from Wilmington University. Sebastian and his family live in Pennsylvania.